Everyday COMFORT FOOD

Everyday COMFORT FOOD

Tasty, warming recipes from the bestselling VJ Cooks

VANYA INSULL

ALLEN&UNWIN
AUCKLAND • SYDNEY • MELBOURNE • LONDON

To my mum, Margot, and my dad, Paul –
thank you for all your love and support.
You've always encouraged me with every
new idea, standing behind me and
cheering me on every step of the way.
I'm so grateful for you both.

CONTENTS

INTRODUCTION

I can't believe we're onto book three already — what an achievement! I've had so much fun putting this one together, and I reckon it perfectly complements my first two books, *Everyday Favourites* and *Summer Favourites*. I like to think of these cookbooks as a trio, covering all seasons. This one is packed with hearty recipes, perfect for warming up those chilly nights with delicious, comforting food.

We had a great time shooting the photos here in Taupō in the middle of winter, with the beautiful trees and rivers as our backdrop. My husband, Mike, is a keen fly fisherman, and we captured some super shots of him in action. I also love seeing the photos of my sons, Archie and Henry, their cheeky personalities showing through as they grow — a little bolder in each cookbook.

In this book I had to have an everyday dinners and classics section, because that's what I'm known for: easy, tasty family meals you can get on the table quickly or with little fuss. After that I've got soups, pies and slow-cooker recipes, so all the winter meal bases are covered.

I've included some of my most popular recipes, along with a few new ones that I know you and your family will love. There's something so satisfying about coming home to the mouth-watering aroma of a slow-cooked dinner, knowing it's going to taste amazing and the hard work is already done.

Some of my personal favourites in this book include the pulled pork pie (page 92), which is full of flavour thanks to the slow-cooked apples, and the spiced lamb (page 32) served with home-made flatbreads. I made the lamb dish at the studio while I was testing the recipe, and my sisters *miraculously* turned up at lunchtime (haha), so we sat down and enjoyed a fabulous lunch. The tender pulled lamb goes perfectly with the feta whip and those garlicky flatbreads!

You'll find plenty of tasty treats in the baking and dessert sections: cookies, cakes, loaves, slices and, of course, puddings. I love a good self-saucing pudding, so I've snuck in three different kinds: berry, ginger and (our family favourite) chocolate.

This year has brought some exciting changes. I've leased a space in central Taupō, where we've created a kitchen studio for recipe testing and office admin. We also launched a meal-planning app, which is helping thousands of people reduce the overwhelm when it comes to that age-old question: 'What's for dinner?' I'm so grateful for the support of my team; we have such a ball creating recipes together and growing this foodie business — I couldn't do it without them.

I appreciate every one of you who has bought one of my books over the past few years. I love the feedback I receive, and meeting people at book signings is always such a highlight! I can't wait to hear what you think of this one . . .

Happy cooking,
VJ x

ABOUT MY RECIPES

For those who are new to my recipes: I'm a busy mum, so I design my recipes to take the stress out of feeding a family. I try to keep them as simple as possible, using everyday ingredients that you probably already have in the pantry or fridge — and that kids are likely to be happy to eat.

Most of my dinner recipes are super-versatile, and I've provided tips on alternative ingredients as well as serving suggestions. Feel free to add or swap in any appropriate vegetables that you have hiding in the back of your fridge. Similarly, some of the baking and dessert recipes in this book call for fresh fruit, but if the fruits listed aren't readily available locally you can usually substitute them with others — or even use canned fruit.

While most of my dinner recipes feed a family of four, a few of them make a larger quantity because I like to freeze extra portions for another meal at a later date. Once the leftovers have cooled to room temperature, I transfer them to an airtight container or sealable bag and freeze them for up to 3 months. When I need a meal in a hurry, I defrost them and reheat until piping hot.

I also love to freeze baking to have on hand for a quick lunchbox filler. Cookie dough, baked muffins and loaves all freeze well, so I often double the recipes and freeze half.

I use fan bake for the majority of my cooking, unless stated otherwise. If you are using a conventional oven instead, the general rule of thumb is to add 20°C (70°F), so for example 180°C (350°F) fan bake would be 200°C (400°F) in a conventional oven. All ovens have their own quirks. You probably already know if yours runs hot or cold, so feel free to adjust the cook times and temperatures accordingly.

When baking, I always line my tins and trays with baking paper. This prevents my baking from sticking to the tin and ensures everything comes out in one piece. It also makes for an easy clean-up.

I specify the size of my baking tins in my recipes, but if your tins are slightly different the recipes will still work! If your tin is larger the bake time will be shorter, whereas if it's smaller it may take longer for your baking to fully cook through. Just keep an eye on the time, and bake until a skewer inserted into your baking comes out clean.

MASTER MEASUREMENTS

I use New Zealand standard measures in my recipes:

1 teaspoon (tsp) = 5 ml (⅙ fl oz)
1 tablespoon (Tbsp) = 15 ml (½ fl oz)
¼ cup of liquid = 60 ml (2 fl oz)
½ cup of liquid = 125 ml (4 fl oz)
1 cup of liquid = 250 ml (9 fl oz)

The weight of a cup of dry ingredients will vary depending on the mass of the ingredients. These are some of the common quantities I use in my baking and this cookbook:

1 cup of plain flour = 150 g (5½ oz)
1 cup of wholemeal flour = 155 g (5⅔ oz)
1 cup of white or caster sugar = 220 g (7¾ oz)
1 cup of brown sugar (firmly packed) = 200 g (7 oz)
1 cup of icing sugar = 130 g (4½ oz)
1 cup of cocoa powder = 90 g (3¼ oz)
1 cup of grated cheese = 100 g (3½ oz)

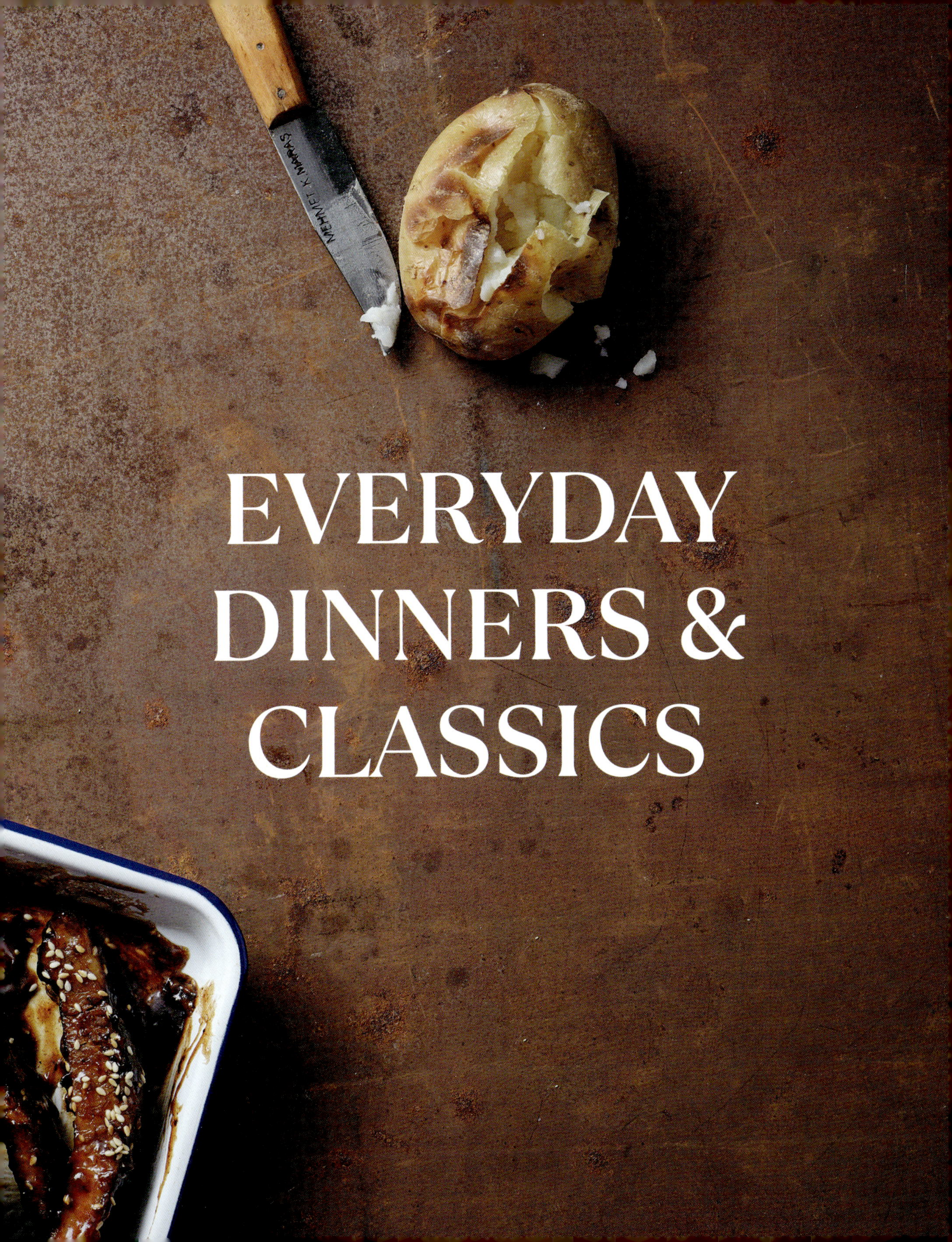

EVERYDAY DINNERS & CLASSICS

WHAT'S IN THIS CHAPTER

Beef Short Ribs p40

Roast Pumpkin, Cauliflower and Chickpea Bowl p44

One-pot Prawn Orzo p46

Roast Chicken on Couscous p48

Creamy Salmon Fillets p50

Barbecue Glazed Meatloaves p54

Chicken Satay Yellow Curry p56

Lebanese Mince on Hummus p58

Oven-baked Lamb Curry p60

BARBECUE CHICKEN RICE BOWLS

I'm always looking for new rice bowl ideas to serve the family, and this barbecue chicken bowl is a great addition to my rotation. The chicken is coated in barbecue sauce then baked in the oven. The barbecue mayo brings all the ingredients together at the end.

Ready in 50 minutes
Serves 4

500 g (1 lb 2 oz) boneless chicken thighs, sliced into strips
½ cup barbecue sauce, plus extra for brushing
1 red capsicum

Bean Mix

420 g (14¾ oz) can corn kernels, rinsed and drained
420 g (14¾ oz) can four bean mix, rinsed and drained
salt and cracked black pepper, to taste

Barbecue Mayo

¼ cup mayonnaise
2 Tbsp barbecue sauce
1 tsp water

To serve

steamed rice
flesh of 1 avocado, diced
1 spring onion, sliced

1. Preheat the oven to 200°C (400°F) fan bake. Line a baking tray with baking paper.
2. Coat the chicken in the barbecue sauce and arrange it on the prepared tray. Chop the capsicum into large pieces and add to the tray.
3. Bake for 25 minutes while you prepare the Bean Mix.
4. To make the Bean Mix, add a dash of oil to a large frying pan. Add the corn and cook over a medium heat until starting to brown. Pour in the beans. Once the beans are heated through, season well with salt and pepper. Remove from the heat.
5. Remove the tray from the oven and set aside the capsicum. Brush extra barbecue sauce over the top of the chicken. Return to the oven for a further 5 minutes until sticky, golden and cooked through.
6. Cut the roasted capsicum into thin slices.
7. To make the Barbecue Mayo, mix together the mayonnaise and barbecue sauce. Add a dash of water so that it is a pouring consistency.
8. Divide the rice among 4 bowls, then top with the hot Bean Mix, capsicum, avocado and sticky chicken pieces. Drizzle over the Barbecue Mayo and scatter over the spring onion. Serve immediately.

QUICK ONE-POT LASAGNE

I absolutely love a one-pot meal. Not only is it quick and easy to prepare, but there is only one pot to wash at the end! Adding ricotta and basil really elevates this from a classic mince and pasta dish.

Ready in 35 minutes
Serves 4

1 Tbsp olive oil
1 onion, finely diced
3 cloves garlic, crushed
2 Tbsp sliced sun-dried tomatoes
500 g (1 lb 2 oz) beef mince
2 tsp dried Italian herbs
1 tsp white sugar
2 Tbsp tomato paste
1 vegetable stock cube
1½ cups boiling water
400 g (14 oz) can crushed tomatoes
400 g (14 oz) fresh lasagne sheets
salt and cracked black pepper, to taste
50 g (1¾ oz) parmesan, grated
150 g (5½ oz) ricotta
fresh basil, for garnish

1. Heat the oil in a large frying pan. Add the onion and sauté for a few minutes. Add the garlic and sun-dried tomatoes and stir for 2 minutes.
2. Add the beef mince and use a spatula to break it up, frying until the mince has browned.
3. Add the Italian herbs, sugar and tomato paste and stir through the mince.
4. Dissolve the stock cube in the boiling water. Add to the pan with the canned tomatoes and stir through the mince.
5. Roughly chop the fresh lasagne sheets into pieces. Add to the pan and stir to coat in the mince mixture.
6. Simmer on low for 10 minutes, until the lasagne sheets have softened and most of the liquid has been absorbed. Season to taste with salt and pepper.
7. Sprinkle over the parmesan and add spoonfuls of the ricotta to the top. Once the cheese has melted, serve immediately with basil to garnish.

Tips + tricks

+ Swap the beef mince for chicken or pork mince.

Kids' fave

APRICOT CHICKEN TRAY BAKE

This recipe may be a little retro, but let me tell you, the flavours are still amazing. The best thing about this meal is how simple it is to prepare. Simply add the ingredients to the baking dish and let the oven do all of the work.

Ready in 1 hour 10 minutes
Serves 6

1 kg (2 lb 4 oz) boneless, skinless chicken thighs
410 g (14½ oz) can apricot halves in juice
1 Tbsp crushed garlic
2 tsp ground cumin
3 Tbsp dark soy sauce
2 Tbsp cornflour
30 g (1 oz) sliced almonds

To serve

steamed white rice
sliced spring onion
steamed green vegetables

1. Preheat the oven to 200°C (400°F) fan bake.
2. Cut each chicken thigh into 3 pieces and add to a large baking dish.
3. Drain the can of apricot halves, reserving the juice for later. Scatter the apricot halves over the chicken.
4. Add the garlic, cumin, soy sauce and cornflour to 100 ml (3½ fl oz) of the reserved apricot juice, and mix together. Pour over the chicken.
5. Bake for 40 minutes.
6. Turn the chicken over and scatter with the almonds.
7. Bake for a further 10 minutes, until the chicken is golden and cooked through.
8. Serve on top of fluffy rice with spring onion to garnish and steamed greens on the side.

Tips + tricks

- Any leftovers can be stored in an airtight container in the freezer for up to 3 months. Reheat until piping hot before serving.
- This could also be served on top of mashed potatoes.

POTATO TOP SAUSAGE BAKE

I am always looking for new ways to cook sausages, and this recipe has been so well received online. The potatoes sit on top of the sausage casserole and soak up the beautiful onion gravy.

Ready in 1 hour 30 minutes
Serves 4–6

1 Tbsp olive oil
500 g (1 lb 2 oz) beef sausages
2 onions, sliced
2 cloves garlic, crushed
1 Tbsp brown sugar
2 Tbsp balsamic vinegar
2 Tbsp butter
2 Tbsp plain flour
1 Tbsp dried mixed herbs
1 beef stock cube
1 cup boiling water
salt and cracked black pepper, to taste

Cheesy Potato Top

2 medium potatoes, thinly sliced
1 cup grated cheese

To serve

chopped fresh Italian parsley
steamed seasonal vegetables or fresh garden salad

1. Preheat the oven to 200°C (400°F) fan bake.
2. Add 1 teaspoon of the oil to a medium cast-iron dish over a medium heat. Add the sausages and brown on all sides. Remove from the dish and set aside.
3. Reduce the heat to low and add the remaining oil, onions and garlic. Gently sauté for a few minutes, until soft.
4. Add the sugar and vinegar, and cook, stirring, for another minute. Add the butter. Once the butter has melted, sprinkle over the flour and mixed herbs and mix to combine.
5. Dissolve the stock cube in the boiling water. Pour into the dish and deglaze the pan. Simmer for 1 minute.
6. Chop the browned sausages and add to the dish, mixing everything together. Season to taste with salt and pepper, then remove from the heat.
7. To make the Cheesy Potato Top, arrange half of the potato slices on top of the sausage mix. Sprinkle over half of the grated cheese. Repeat the layers with the remaining potato slices and cheese.
8. Cover the dish with a lid or tinfoil and bake for 40 minutes.
9. Remove the lid or tinfoil and cook for a further 20 minutes until the cheese is golden and the potatoes are cooked through.
10. Scatter with parsley and serve immediately with steamed vegetables or a salad.

PORK CHOPS WITH MUSHROOM SAUCE

This is a tasty and slightly different way to have pork chops. The mushroom sauce has a nice sweetness to it with the red onion, and the fresh thyme goes well with the tender, juicy chops.

Ready in 30 minutes
Serves 4

800 g (1 lb 12 oz) pork chops
salt and cracked black pepper, to season
1 tsp paprika
1 Tbsp butter
1 Tbsp olive oil
1 red onion, sliced
1 cup vegetable stock
250 g (9 oz) mushrooms, sliced
4 cloves garlic, crushed
½ cup cream

To serve

1 Tbsp fresh thyme
mashed potatoes
steamed green vegetables

1. Trim the skin off the pork chops, leaving a thin layer of fat. Season with salt and pepper and sprinkle over the paprika.
2. Heat the butter and oil in a large skillet or non-stick frying pan. Once hot and bubbling, sear the pork chops for 4 minutes per side until golden brown.
3. Remove the pork chops and cover to keep warm. If the chops are thick, add them to a warm oven while you make the sauce.
4. Add the red onion to the pan. Pour in half of the stock and stir to deglaze the pan. Add the mushrooms and stir to combine. Stir in the garlic and cook for 2 minutes.
5. Pour in the remaining stock and the cream. Bring to a gentle simmer for 5 minutes until the sauce has reduced and thickened up. Season to taste with salt and pepper.
6. Return the pork chops and their juices to the sauce and allow to reheat for 2–3 minutes.
7. Serve garnished with thyme on top of mashed potatoes with steamed greens.

SLOW-ROASTED PULLED LAMB

This is such an epic meal to make if you're entertaining. The lamb takes on so much flavour from the spiced marinade. Serve the meat, whipped feta and fresh veggies on my amazing Home-made Flatbreads (see page 34).

Ready in 4 hours + marinating time
Serves 6+

Spiced Marinade

2 tsp dried oregano
2 tsp ground cumin
2 tsp ground coriander
1 tsp cinnamon
1 tsp salt
½ tsp white pepper
1 Tbsp chopped fresh rosemary
2 cloves garlic, crushed
3 Tbsp olive oil

1.5–2 kg (3 lb 5 oz–4 lb 8 oz) lamb shoulder or leg
2 onions, quartered
2 cups water

Feta Whip

50 g (1¾ oz) feta
⅓ cup Greek yoghurt
1 Tbsp lemon juice
salt and cracked black pepper, to taste

To serve

6 Home-made Flatbreads (see page 34)
30 g (1 oz) rocket leaves
100 g (3½ oz) cherry tomatoes, halved
chopped fresh mint

1. To make the Spiced Marinade, combine all the ingredients in a bowl. Coat the lamb on all sides with the marinade. Marinate in the fridge for at least 1 hour or preferably overnight.
2. Preheat the oven to 160°C (315°F) fan bake.
3. Place the onion quarters in a large oven dish. Place the marinated lamb on top of the onions and pour half the water into the dish. Cover with a lid or tinfoil and roast for 2 hours.
4. Remove the lid and add the remaining water. Roast for a further 1–1.5 hours until the lamb is tender and pulls apart easily.
5. While the lamb is cooking, make the Feta Whip. Mix together all the ingredients until smooth and well combined. Chill until ready to use.
6. Serve the pulled lamb on Home-made Flatbreads, topped with rocket, tomatoes and Feta Whip, with mint sprinkled on top.

Tips + tricks

+ Lamb shoulder is preferred for its tenderness and flavour, but lamb leg works well too.
+ Keep an eye on the water level in the oven dish. To prevent the lamb from drying out, add more water if necessary.
+ The Feta Whip can be made a day ahead and stored in an airtight container in the fridge.

HOME-MADE FLATBREADS

Not only are these flatbreads easy to make, but they are the best I have ever tasted. Be warned, though: after making these once we've never gone back to store-bought flatbreads! These are so good for dipping into curries (like the ones on pages 56, 60 and 112), mopping up sauces or holding grilled meats. The garlic butter is optional depending on how you are serving them.

Ready in 20 minutes
Makes 6

1¼ cups Greek yoghurt
2 cups plain flour
2 tsp baking powder
1 tsp salt
1 tsp olive oil

Garlic Butter (optional)
30 g (1 oz) butter, melted
1 clove garlic, crushed
1 Tbsp finely chopped Italian parsley

1. Add the yoghurt, flour, baking powder and salt to a large bowl. Mix to combine.
2. On a well-floured bench, knead the mixture a few times to form a smooth dough.
3. Cut the dough into 6 pieces. Using a well-floured rolling pin, roll each piece out into a circle.
4. Heat the oil in a frying pan over a medium-high heat and cook each flatbread for a few minutes on each side until golden brown. Transfer the cooked flatbreads to a plate and keep warm until ready to use.
5. If making the Garlic Butter, combine all the ingredients and brush over the cooked flatbreads.

Tips + tricks

+ These are best eaten on the day they are made.
+ You can prepare the dough in advance and keep it in the fridge for up to 24 hours. Just bring it to room temperature before rolling out and cooking.

STICKY PORK RIBS WITH BAKED POTATOES

Growing up, I loved going to Lone Star as a family and we would always order the pork ribs. With this recipe you can create amazing ribs at home, served alongside my easy oven-baked potatoes. This meal is all about minimum fuss and maximum flavour.

Ready in 1 hour 40 minutes + chilling time
Serves 4

Barbecue Marinade

¼ cup barbecue sauce
2 Tbsp soy sauce
2 Tbsp sweet chilli sauce
2 Tbsp honey
1 Tbsp garlic powder
1 Tbsp sesame seeds

1.2 kg (2 lb 10 oz) pork ribs
4 large potatoes
salt, to season
1 tsp sesame seeds, to garnish
4 tsp butter
4 Tbsp sour cream
1 bag pre-made coleslaw

1. To make the Barbecue Marinade, combine all the ingredients in a large container. Add the pork ribs and coat in the marinade. Cover and chill for at least 1 hour or overnight.
2. Preheat the oven to 170°C (325°F) fan bake.
3. Add the ribs to a baking dish and cover with a lid or tinfoil. Place all 4 potatoes on one long piece of tinfoil, season with salt and wrap up tightly. Place the ribs in the oven and the potatoes on the oven rack above.
4. Bake for 1½ hours.
5. Remove the baking dish from the oven and use a sharp knife and tongs to carefully separate the ribs. Brush over any sauce from the bottom of the dish. Turn the oven up to 200°C (400°F) and bake uncovered for 15 minutes until the ribs are caramelised and sticky.
6. Drizzle any extra sauce from the baking dish over the ribs or brush over extra barbecue sauce if they are looking dry. Sprinkle the sesame seeds over the top.
7. Remove the baked potatoes from the oven and carefully open the tinfoil. Cut an X shape in the top of each one, then add 1 teaspoon of butter and 1 tablespoon of sour cream to each one.
8. Serve the ribs hot with the baked potatoes and coleslaw.

Tips + tricks

+ I like to serve my ribs with baked potatoes but oven wedges or fries would be delicious too.
+ If possible, it's a good idea to prepare and marinate the ribs the night before.

Kids' fave

COUNTRY CHICKEN POTATO BAKE

This recipe was a happy accident of sorts. I thought I was grabbing a can of corn kernels and I didn't realise until I got home it was creamed corn. This made the casserole creamy and tasty. Oven-roasted potatoes and grated cheese are added and grilled to make a golden topping.

Ready in 1 hour
Serves 6

Roasted Potato Topping

600 g (1 lb 5 oz) potatoes, peeled
1 tsp olive oil
salt, to season
1 fresh rosemary sprig, leaves chopped
½ cup grated Colby cheese
20 g (¾ oz) parmesan, grated

1 tsp olive oil
1 onion, diced
2 carrots, peeled and diced
2 stalks celery, sliced
1 kg (2 lb 4 oz) boneless chicken thighs
100 g (3½ oz) mushrooms, halved
2 cloves garlic, crushed
400 g (14 oz) can creamed corn
1 cup boiling water
30 g (1 oz) packet French onion soup
1 tsp dried mixed herbs

To serve

steamed seasonal green vegetables or salad

1. Preheat the oven to 200°C (400°F) fan bake. Line a baking tray with baking paper.
2. To make the Roasted Potato Topping, dice the potatoes into 1 cm (½ in) cubes and place on the prepared tray. Drizzle with the oil, season with salt and scatter over the rosemary.
3. Bake for 20 minutes while you prepare the filling.
4. Heat the oil in a large frying pan over a medium heat. Add the onion, carrots and celery. Cook for 5 minutes.
5. Cut the chicken thighs into bite-sized pieces, then add to the pan. Add the mushrooms and garlic. Cook, while stirring, for a further 5 minutes.
6. Add the corn, boiling water, onion soup and mixed herbs to the pan. Stir together until combined, then remove from the heat. Transfer to a large baking dish and place in the oven.
7. Give the roasted potatoes a shake and return the tray to the oven. Bake on the rack below the filling for 20 minutes.
8. Remove the filling from the oven and give it a stir. Remove the roasted potatoes and spread them over the top of the filling. Sprinkle over the cheese and parmesan.
9. Turn the oven to the grill setting. Grill for 5–10 minutes until the cheese is golden and bubbling. Be careful not to let the topping burn.
10. Serve immediately with a side of steamed greens or salad.

Tips + tricks

+ You can swap the French onion soup for your favourite type of packet soup.

BEEF SHORT RIBS

Beef short ribs are one of my favourite things to order at a restaurant, so I really enjoyed recreating them at home. These ribs are super-tender and so tasty. A great special-occasion dish to impress your guests.

Ready in 3 hours 15 minutes
Serves 4

1.4 kg (3 lb 2 oz) beef short ribs
salt and cracked black pepper, to season
1 Tbsp plain flour
1 Tbsp olive oil
1 onion, finely diced
1 carrot, peeled and finely chopped
1 beef stock cube
1½ cups boiling water
1 Tbsp balsamic vinegar
1 cup red wine
1 Tbsp brown sugar

To serve
mashed potatoes
steamed green vegetables

1. Preheat the oven to 170°C (325°F) fan bake.
2. Season the ribs well with salt and pepper, then coat in the flour.
3. Heat the oil in an ovenproof casserole dish. Add the ribs and brown on all sides. Remove from the pan and set aside.
4. In the same pan, sauté the onion and carrot until soft.
5. Dissolve the stock cube in the boiling water. Add to the pan with the vinegar. Stir in the wine and sugar. Return the ribs to the pan and cover with the lid or tinfoil.
6. Bake for 3 hours or until the meat is falling apart, turning halfway through.
7. Serve on mashed potatoes with a side of greens. Spoon any extra sauce from the dish over the top.

Tips + tricks

+ You may need to add a splash of water during the cook time if the sauce is becoming too thick.
+ Beef cheeks can be used instead of short ribs. If using beef cheeks, bake for 2–3 hours until the meat falls apart.

ROAST PUMPKIN, CAULIFLOWER AND CHICKPEA BOWL

If you're looking for a healthy and nourishing dinner or lunch, this is it. I love the taste and texture of the crispy roasted chickpeas and cauliflower. With your favourite hummus and an egg added on top, there is no shortage of punchy flavours here.

Ready in 50 minutes
Serves 4

¼ pumpkin, peeled
3 Tbsp olive oil
1 Tbsp maple syrup
1 tsp ground cumin
1 tsp garlic powder
1 tsp flaky sea salt
400 g (14 oz) can chickpeas, rinsed and drained
½ cauliflower, chopped
1 cup brown rice
200 g (7 oz) haloumi, sliced

To serve

flesh of 1 avocado, sliced
4 Tbsp hummus
4 eggs, poached or fried
1 tsp sesame seeds
chopped fresh herbs
1 tsp balsamic glaze (optional)

1. Preheat the oven to 200°C (400°F) fan bake. Line 2 baking trays with baking paper.
2. Dice the pumpkin into 1 cm (½ in) cubes. Add to one of the prepared trays and drizzle over 1 tablespoon of the oil and the maple syrup. Stir to coat.
3. Add the cumin, garlic powder, salt and 1 tablespoon of the oil to a large bowl and mix to combine. Add the chickpeas and stir to coat. Pour onto half of the second prepared tray.
4. Add the cauliflower to the same bowl and stir to coat in the oil and spices left in the bowl. Transfer the cauliflower to the other half of the tray.
5. Place both trays in the oven and bake for 30 minutes.
6. Cook the brown rice according to the packet instructions.
7. Add the remaining oil to a frying pan. Pan-fry the haloumi for a few minutes on each side until golden, then cut into bite-sized pieces.
8. Divide the brown rice among 4 bowls, then top with the roasted pumpkin, cauliflower and chickpeas. Add haloumi pieces, avocado, hummus and an egg to each bowl. Sprinkle over sesame seeds and fresh herbs, and serve with a drizzle of balsamic glaze (if using).

Tips + tricks

+ I poached my eggs but you can fry or boil them instead — or leave them off if you prefer.
+ Kūmara, capsicum, zucchini or broccoli would all make great swaps for the pumpkin and cauliflower.

ONE-POT PRAWN ORZO

This is an amazing one-pot meal where all the beautiful cooking juices help to infuse the orzo with flavour. If you're a fan of paella, you will love the prawn and chorizo combination. The cream cheese at the end really brings the dish together.

Ready in 35 minutes
Serves 6

2 Tbsp olive oil
1 onion, finely diced
2 cloves garlic, crushed
160 g (5¾ oz) chorizo, finely chopped
500 g (1 lb 2 oz) dried orzo pasta
2 vegetable stock cubes
3 cups boiling water
400 g (14 oz) can cherry tomatoes
300 g (10½ oz) prawns, thawed with tails removed
100 g (3½ oz) cream cheese
1 cup frozen peas, thawed
25 g (1 oz) parmesan, grated, plus extra for garnish
salt and cracked black pepper, to taste
fresh basil, for garnish

1. Heat a large non-stick frying pan over a low heat. Add the oil, onion, garlic and chorizo and gently sauté for a few minutes.
2. Pour in the orzo and mix to combine. Cook for 2 minutes to toast the orzo.
3. Dissolve the stock cubes in the boiling water, then pour into the pan to deglaze it. Add the canned tomatoes and mix to combine.
4. Simmer for about 15 minutes until most of the liquid has been absorbed and the orzo is almost cooked. Keep stirring to prevent the orzo from sticking to the bottom of the pan.
5. Add the prawns and cream cheese. Stir until the cream cheese has melted and the prawns are cooked through.
6. Stir in the peas and parmesan. Once the orzo is al dente, season to taste with salt and pepper.
7. Grate over the extra parmesan and garnish with basil. Serve immediately.

Tips + tricks

+ I used a mild chorizo but if you like a bit of heat use a spicy version instead.
+ Swap the frozen peas for baby spinach.
+ If you don't like prawns, leave them out and add extra chorizo.
+ Make a chicken version by swapping the chorizo for diced chicken thighs.

ROAST CHICKEN ON COUSCOUS

An alternative to the classic roast chook, this tasty meal involves cooking a chicken on a bed of vegetables. As you add the various layers, the chicken continues to cook while its juices flavour everything in the dish. A real winner!

Ready in 2 hours 5 minutes
Serves 4

1 red onion, sliced into wedges
1 Tbsp olive oil
1 lemon, halved
1.8 kg (4 lb) whole chicken
1 carrot, peeled and diced
1 red capsicum, sliced
200 g (7 oz) cherry tomatoes
1 chicken stock cube
1 cup boiling water
1 cup couscous

To serve
chopped fresh Italian parsley
lemon wedges

1. Preheat the oven to 180°C (350°F) fan bake.
2. In the bottom of a large cast-iron casserole dish, add the red onion and drizzle with the oil. Place the lemon halves in the dish and set the chicken on top.
3. Cover with a lid or tinfoil and bake for 1 hour.
4. Remove from the oven, take off the lid or tinfoil and set the chicken aside. Stir the carrot, capsicum and tomatoes through the onion and chicken juices. Place the chicken back on top.
5. Bake uncovered for a further 30–45 minutes, until the chicken is cooked through.
6. Remove the chicken and place on a board. Cover with tinfoil and set aside to rest.
7. Squeeze the juice from the roasted lemon halves into the dish, then discard (careful, the lemon halves will be hot). Dissolve the stock cube in the boiling water, then pour it and the couscous over the vegetables and stir together. Cover with the lid or tinfoil.
8. Bake for a further 5 minutes.
9. Remove the dish from the oven and stir. Leave to sit on the bench, covered, for 10 minutes while the couscous absorbs all of the liquid.
10. Cut the chicken into pieces. Serve on top of the roast vegetables and couscous with a sprinkle of parsley and some lemon wedges to squeeze over.

CREAMY SALMON FILLETS

This is a truly delicious way to enjoy fresh salmon fillets. The herb, lemon and garlic sauce is perfect served with some mashed potatoes or crusty bread to mop up all of the flavours. This is also tasty with pasta or steamed rice.

Ready in 30 minutes
Serves 4

600 g (1 lb 5 oz) salmon fillet
salt and cracked black pepper, to season
1 Tbsp olive oil
1 onion, finely diced
1 Tbsp butter
2 cloves garlic, crushed
2 tsp plain flour
1 vegetable stock cube
1 cup boiling water
½ cup cream
zest and juice of 1 lemon
1 tsp dried Italian herbs
25 g (1 oz) parmesan, grated

To serve
chopped fresh Italian parsley
lemon wedges

1. Cut the salmon into 4 equal portions and pat dry. Season with salt and pepper.
2. Place a large frying pan over a medium heat and add the oil. Place the salmon skin-side up. Sear for 5 minutes until golden.
3. Carefully remove the salmon and set aside, leaving the oil in the pan.
4. In the same pan, add the onion and sauté for 1 minute. Add the butter and garlic and stir to combine. Sprinkle over the flour and fry off.
5. Dissolve the stock cube in the boiling water, then pour into the pan and simmer for 1 minute. Pour in the cream. Add the lemon zest and juice, Italian herbs and parmesan. Simmer, while stirring, for a few minutes.
6. Carefully place the salmon back in the pan, skin-side down. Place a lid on top and cook over a low heat for a further 5 minutes, or until the salmon is cooked through.
7. Sprinkle with parsley and serve immediately with lemon wedges to squeeze over.

BARBECUE GLAZED MEATLOAVES

Over the years of running my website this has been one of the most requested recipes. Given its popularity I knew it would be perfect for this cookbook. The recipe makes two meatloaves, which means you can freeze one for another day — because who doesn't like to get ahead?!

Ready in 1 hour
Makes 2 meatloaves; each serves 4

Meatloaves

2 onions, finely chopped
1 carrot, peeled and finely grated
1 kg (2 lb 4 oz) beef mince
450 g (1 lb) sausage meat
2 Tbsp dried mixed herbs
2 eggs
1 Tbsp crushed garlic
2 Tbsp Worcestershire sauce
2 tsp salt
1 cup dried breadcrumbs

Barbecue Glaze

½ cup barbecue sauce
2 Tbsp brown sugar
1 Tbsp Worcestershire sauce

To serve

chopped fresh Italian parsley
mashed potatoes
steamed green vegetables

1. Preheat the oven to 180°C (350°F) fan bake. Line 2 loaf tins with baking paper, ensuring one has a generous amount of overhang to fold over the meatloaf for the freezer.
2. To make the Meatloaves, add all the ingredients to a large bowl. Using your hands or a spoon, mix everything until well combined.
3. Divide the mixture evenly between the prepared tins. Spread the mixture out and firmly press down.
4. To make the Barbecue Glaze, mix together all the ingredients in a small jug. Pour half the glaze over each of the meatloaves, spreading it out to the edges.
5. Place one meatloaf in the oven and bake for 45 minutes or until cooked through. Garnish with parsley and serve with mashed potatoes and steamed greens on the side.
6. Fold the extra baking paper over the top of the uncooked meatloaf and place the tin in the freezer. Once frozen, remove the meatloaf from the tin (leave the baking paper on if you like) and wrap in cling film, tinfoil or a bread bag. Store in the freezer for up to 3 months.

Tips + tricks

+ When ready to use the frozen meatloaf, defrost it completely then add back to a lined loaf tin and cook as above.
+ Make sure you are using fresh mince so you are not freezing it twice.
+ You can use the filling of your favourite sausages squeezed from the casings instead of buying sausage meat.

CHICKEN SATAY YELLOW CURRY

Thai yellow curry paste is one of my favourites to use when cooking for my family. It's on the mild side but still gives a great flavour to the dish. Ready in just 20 minutes, this is an ideal mid-week meal.

Ready in 20 minutes
Serves 4

500 g (1 lb 2 oz) boneless chicken thighs
2 tsp sesame oil
salt and cracked black pepper, to season
1 red onion, sliced
2 cloves garlic, crushed
2 Tbsp yellow curry paste
3 Tbsp crunchy peanut butter
1 Tbsp brown sugar
400 ml (14 fl oz) can coconut cream
¼ cup water
1 head broccoli
2 carrots, peeled

To serve
steamed rice
chopped fresh coriander
sliced fresh chilli
lime wedges (optional)

1. Cut each chicken thigh into 3 pieces. Coat the pieces with 1 teaspoon of the sesame oil and season well with salt and pepper.
2. Add the red onion and remaining sesame oil to a large frying pan and sauté for a few minutes. Add the chicken pieces and brown for a few minutes on each side.
3. Make a gap in the centre of the pan and add the garlic, curry paste, peanut butter, sugar and coconut cream. Stir to combine with the chicken and onion. Cook for a few minutes until it starts to thicken up, then add the water.
4. Chop the broccoli into small thin pieces. Use a peeler to make thin ribbons of the carrots. Add both to the pan and stir to combine. Cover with a lid and simmer for 5 minutes or until the broccoli is tender and the chicken is cooked through. Season to taste with salt and pepper.
5. Serve on top of steamed rice with coriander, chilli and lime wedges (if using).

Kids' fave

LEBANESE MINCE ON HUMMUS

This is a tasty and interesting way to cook beef mince. The spiced mince is served on hummus, with pine nuts and fresh herbs sprinkled on top. If you're short on time, you can swap the home-made hummus for a tub of your favourite store-bought kind. Likewise, you can buy flatbreads instead of making your own.

Ready in 30 minutes
Serves 4 as a main or 8 as a shared starter

Home-made Hummus

400 g (14 oz) can chickpeas, rinsed and drained
2 cloves garlic
2 Tbsp lemon juice
2 Tbsp tahini
½ tsp salt
3 Tbsp water

Spiced Mince

1 tsp olive oil
1 onion, finely diced
2 cloves garlic, crushed
500 g (1 lb 2 oz) beef mince
½ tsp allspice
1 tsp ground cumin
1 tsp ground coriander
1 tsp salt
¼ tsp cracked black pepper

To serve

30 g (1 oz) pine nuts, toasted
chopped fresh Italian parsley and mint
Home-made Flatbreads (see page 34, or use store-bought)
rocket leaves
olive oil or chilli oil

1. To make the Home-made Hummus, add the chickpeas, garlic, lemon juice, tahini and salt to a food processor. Add the water, 1 tablespoon at a time, blending until a smooth, creamy consistency is achieved. Set aside while you prepare the mince.
2. To make the Spiced Mince, heat the oil in a frying pan over a medium heat. Add the onion and sauté for a few minutes.
3. Add the garlic and cook for 1 minute.
4. Add the mince and cook, stirring, for 5 minutes or until browned.
5. Add the spices and salt and pepper and cook for 2 minutes.
6. Place the Home-made Hummus on a large plate and spread out to the edges. Top with the Spiced Mince and pine nuts, and garnish with parsley and mint.
7. Serve immediately with warm flatbreads, rocket and a drizzle of olive or chilli oil.

Tips + tricks

+ I use lean beef mince to avoid the mince getting too oily.
+ For a festive twist, add some pomegranate seeds to the garnish.
+ Honey can also be drizzled over the top for a sweet touch.

OVEN-BAKED LAMB CURRY

This dish is actually based on a goat curry that I had at a friend's wedding in Rotorua many years ago. I asked the chef (the bride's brother) for the recipe, which he generously shared, and I've been making this smaller lamb version at home ever since. Feel free to use goat meat instead if you can get your hands on some!

Ready in 2 hours 10 minutes
Serves 8

¾ cup tomato paste
1 cup natural yoghurt
4 tsp garam masala
½ tsp cayenne pepper (optional)
2 Tbsp crushed garlic
1 cup mango chutney
1 Tbsp salt
1 Tbsp white sugar
2 kg (4 lb 8 oz) diced lamb leg (see tips)
2 cups boiling water
½ cup cream

To serve
steamed rice
roti
fresh coriander

1. Preheat the oven to 180°C (350°F) fan bake.
2. Add the tomato paste, yoghurt, garam masala, cayenne pepper (if using), garlic, mango chutney, salt and sugar to a large ovenproof casserole dish over a medium heat. Mix everything together. Cook for 5 minutes, stirring occasionally.
3. Add the lamb and stir until well coated. Pour in the water, mix and cover with a lid or tinfoil.
4. Bake in the oven for 2–2½ hours until the lamb is tender and falling apart.
5. Remove the lid. Scoop off and discard any fat that has risen to the top. Stir in the cream and return to the oven for 5 minutes to heat through.
6. Serve with steamed rice, crispy roti and coriander on top.

Tips + tricks

+ If you prefer a mild curry, leave out the cayenne pepper.
+ I used a leg of lamb that I got on special at the supermarket. But you can use your favourite cut of lamb or even diced lamb.
+ This can also be made with beef, goat or chicken. For a chicken version, reduce the cook time to about 1 hour (making sure the chicken is cooked through).

DELICIOUS SOUPS

WHAT'S IN THIS CHAPTER

CHICKEN NOODLE SOUP

This is an easy chicken soup, ideal if you have someone in your family who isn't feeling well or if you want a warming meal on a cold, wintery night.

Ready in 40 minutes
Serves 4–6

1 Tbsp olive oil
1 onion, finely sliced
3 stalks celery, roughly chopped
2 carrots, peeled and sliced
500 g (1 lb 2 oz) skinless, bone-in chicken thighs
2 litres (70 fl oz) salt-reduced chicken stock
80 g (2¾ oz) dried egg noodles
salt and cracked black pepper, to taste

To serve
chopped fresh Italian parsley

1. Heat the oil in a large pot over a low heat. Add the onion, celery and carrots and gently sauté for a few minutes.
2. Place the chicken thighs in the pot and pour over the stock. Simmer for 30 minutes or until the chicken is cooked through and comes away from the bone easily.
3. Remove the thighs from the pot and place on a chopping board.
4. Add the noodles to the pot to cook while you shred the chicken.
5. Using two forks, pull the chicken apart. Discard the bones and place the shredded chicken in the pot.
6. Once the noodles have cooked through, season the soup to taste with salt and pepper. Serve garnished with parsley.

Tips + tricks

+ I use bone-in chicken thighs to give the soup even more flavour and nutrients. You can use boneless thighs, or even chicken breast if you have it to hand.
+ Another nutritious addition is half a bag of baby spinach. Add the spinach at the same time as the shredded chicken, and serve the soup just after the spinach has wilted.

Kids' fave

FRENCH ONION SOUP

I love a French onion soup. The pieces of bread with grilled Gruyère cheese on top are so good — just the thing for mopping up the rich broth.

Ready in 1 hour 15 minutes
Serves 6

50 g (1¾ oz) butter
1 kg (2 lb 4 oz) brown onions, sliced
1 tsp salt
¾ cup dry white wine
3 Tbsp plain flour
1.5 litres (52 fl oz) beef stock
1 tsp dried thyme
2 bay leaves
2 cloves garlic, crushed
salt and cracked black pepper, to taste

To serve

1 baguette or rustic white loaf
150 g (5½ oz) Gruyère cheese, grated

1. Add the butter, onions and salt to a large pot over a low heat and sauté for 25 minutes, until the onions are golden brown and caramelised. Towards the end, turn down the heat and stir regularly to prevent burning on the bottom of the pot.
2. Add the wine and use a wooden spoon to deglaze the pot. Add the flour and mix well. Pour in the stock and stir in the thyme, bay leaves and garlic. Season to taste with salt and pepper. Bring to a simmer and cook for 30 minutes.
3. Preheat the oven to 180°C (350°F) fan grill. Line a baking tray with baking paper.
4. Slice the bread and lightly brown in the toaster. Place on the prepared tray and top with the cheese. Grill for a few minutes until the cheese is melted and golden brown.
5. Remove the bay leaves from the soup.
6. Serve the soup hot with the cheesy bread on top (or on the side if you want to keep it crispy!).

Tips + tricks

+ You can use 3 beef stock cubes for the stock if you like.
+ If you have extra time, caramelise the onions on a lower heat for a longer time. This will enhance the flavour.

TOMATO SOUP

You won't believe all the flavours that are packed into this tomato soup, which is made from canned crushed tomatoes. It's great to be able to whip up something so delicious from pantry staples.

Ready in 1 hour
Serves 6

50 g (1¾ oz) butter
1 onion, finely diced
2 stalks celery, finely diced
3 cloves garlic, crushed
2 × 400 g (14 oz) cans crushed tomatoes
½ cup chopped fresh basil
1 Tbsp brown sugar
2 cups chicken stock
40 g (1½ oz) parmesan, grated
½ cup cream
salt and cracked black pepper, to taste

To serve
olive oil
cream
grated parmesan
fresh basil
crusty bread, buttered

1. Place a large pot over a medium heat and add the butter, onion and celery. Sauté for 10 minutes until the onion starts to turn translucent.
2. Add the garlic and cook, stirring, for a few more minutes.
3. Add the crushed tomatoes, basil, sugar and stock and stir to combine. Bring to the boil, then reduce to a simmer for 20 minutes.
4. Blend the soup in batches in a heat-resistant blender, or use a stick blender.
5. Once blended to your desired consistency, add the parmesan and cream. Stir until the parmesan has melted. Season to taste with salt and pepper.
6. Serve warm, topped with your choice of oil, cream, parmesan and/or basil, alongside bread for dipping.

Tips + tricks

+ Crushed tomatoes are perfect for this recipe. Try to use unflavoured tomatoes so that they don't add a different flavour to the soup.
+ Take care when blending the soup. Some blenders won't take hot liquids, so if you don't have a heat-resistant blender allow the soup to cool slightly first, or use a stick blender. When removing the blender lid, be careful of any steam.

MUSHROOM SOUP

This is a great recipe to make when you can find mushrooms on special. I like to keep some of the cooked mushrooms aside so I can garnish the soup with fresh thyme, cream and sliced mushrooms at the end.

Ready in 30 minutes
Serves 4

2 Tbsp butter
1 onion, finely chopped
500 g (1 lb 2 oz) mushrooms, sliced
1 tsp fresh thyme, plus extra to serve
2 cloves garlic, crushed
1 litre (35 fl oz) vegetable stock
1 large potato, peeled and diced
100 ml (3½ fl oz) cream, plus extra to serve
salt and cracked black pepper, to taste

1. Add the butter and onion to a large pot over a low heat. Sauté for 2 minutes until the onion is soft.
2. Add the mushrooms and sauté for a further 5 minutes. Set aside ¼ cup of the mushrooms to use as a garnish.
3. Add the thyme and garlic and gently cook for 2 minutes, taking care not to burn the garlic.
4. Pour in the stock to deglaze the pot. Add the potato and simmer for 12 minutes until cooked through.
5. Blend the soup in batches in a heat-resistant blender, or use a stick blender. Add the blitzed mixture back to the pot. Pour in the cream.
6. Place the pot over a low heat and gently heat. Season to taste with salt and pepper.
7. Serve with a drizzle of cream, garnished with the reserved mushrooms and thyme.

Tips + tricks

+ Take care when blending the soup. Some blenders won't take hot liquids, so if you don't have a heat-resistant blender allow the soup to cool slightly first, or use a stick blender. When removing the blender lid, be careful of any steam.

BACON HOCK AND BARLEY SOUP

This soup reminds me of my grandma Bonnie. She used to come over to Rotorua from Tauranga when I was a kid, and she would always bring this soup in her thermos. It's super-easy, all made in the slow cooker and has the beautiful, salty flavours of the bacon hock.

Ready in 6 hours 30 minutes
Serves 6

800 g (1 lb 12 oz) bacon hock
1 onion, finely sliced
½ cup barley
2 litres (70 fl oz) water
3 carrots, peeled and sliced
3 stalks celery, sliced
2 bay leaves
salt and cracked black pepper, to taste

To serve
chopped fresh Italian parsley

1. Place the bacon hock, onion, barley, water, carrots, celery and bay leaves in the base of a large slow cooker.
2. Cook on high for 6+ hours until the meat is cooked through and falling off the bone.
3. Remove the hock from the slow cooker and place on a chopping board. Shred the meat, discarding any skin and bones.
4. Place the shredded meat back into the slow cooker and stir to combine. Remove the bay leaves.
5. Season to taste with salt and pepper. Serve in bowls with parsley on top.

Tips + tricks

+ Barley can be substituted with split peas, packet soup mix or dried lentils.

CORN AND POTATO CHOWDER

**This is a tasty vegetarian soup that freezes well.
I love a chowder and this one is hearty and delicious!**

Ready in 50 minutes
Serves 6

1 Tbsp butter
1 onion, finely diced
2 stalks celery, finely diced
1 tsp dried mixed herbs
½ tsp smoked paprika
4 cups frozen corn
2 large potatoes, peeled and diced
1 litre (35 fl oz) vegetable (or chicken) stock
½ cup cream
salt and cracked black pepper, to taste

To serve
chopped chives
sour cream

1. Melt the butter in a large pot over a low heat. Add the onion and celery and sauté for 5 minutes.
2. Stir in the mixed herbs, paprika, corn and potatoes. Pour over the stock and stir to combine. Bring to the boil.
3. Reduce the heat to a simmer. Simmer for 20 minutes or until the potatoes are tender and cooked through, stirring every few minutes.
4. Pour in the cream and stir to combine. Season to taste with salt and pepper.
5. Scoop 3 cups of the soup out and into a heat-resistant blender. Blend until smooth, then pour the blended soup back into the pot.
6. Serve immediately, garnished with chives and a dollop of sour cream.

Tips + tricks

+ Take care when blending the soup. Some blenders won't take hot liquids, so if you don't have a heat-resistant blender allow the soup to cool slightly first. When removing the blender lid, be careful of any steam.
+ This soup can be frozen in an airtight container for up to 3 months.

DUMPLING NOODLE SOUP

The great thing about this meal is that you use pre-made frozen dumplings, and you just make a tasty broth to cook the dumplings in. This is a spicy, warming soup that you'll love in winter.

Ready in 25 minutes
Serves 4

Broth
3 cloves garlic, crushed
2.5 cm (1 in) piece fresh ginger, grated
2 chicken stock cubes
2 tsp sesame oil
2 tsp white sugar
3 Tbsp soy sauce
2 litres (70 fl oz) boiling water

16 pre-made frozen dumplings (flavour of your choice)
2 bunches bok choy
400 g (14 oz) fresh egg noodles

To serve
1 fresh red chilli, sliced
2 spring onions, sliced
chopped fresh coriander (optional)

1. To make the Broth, add all the ingredients to a large pot over a high heat and bring to the boil.
2. Add the dumplings to the pot and simmer for 5 minutes while you prepare the bok choy.
3. Cut the bok choy in half and wash well under water.
4. Add the bok choy and noodles to the pot and cook for 2 minutes.
5. To serve, use tongs to transfer the dumplings to bowls. Add the noodles and bok choy, then ladle over the hot broth. Top with the chilli, spring onions and coriander (if using). Serve immediately.

Tips + tricks

+ You can find pre-made dumplings in the freezer at the supermarket. I used pork and prawn dumplings but any flavour will work.
+ Use your favourite greens or vegetables to customise this noodle soup.

SEAFOOD CHOWDER

My husband Mike is a huge fan of seafood chowder so I thought it was time to recreate it at home. This one is nice and creamy, perfect served with crusty bread and garnished with fresh chives.

Ready in 40 minutes
Serves 6

1 Tbsp butter
1 onion, finely chopped
1 stalk celery, finely chopped
1 clove garlic, crushed
3 cups fish stock
3 medium potatoes, peeled and diced
3 Tbsp cornflour
1 cup cream
500 g (1 lb 2 oz) marinara mix
250 g (9 oz) prawns, tails removed
2 Tbsp chopped fresh Italian parsley

To serve

crusty bread
lemon wedges
chopped chives (optional)

1. Heat a large pot over a low heat. Add the butter, onion, celery and garlic and sauté for a few minutes until soft.
2. Add the stock and potatoes. Simmer for 10 minutes.
3. Whisk the cornflour into the cream and pour into the pot. Bring to a simmer.
4. Add the marinara mix and prawns and stir to combine. Simmer for 5–10 minutes until the seafood is cooked through and the chowder has thickened up.
5. Just before serving, stir through the parsley.
6. Serve with crusty bread and lemon wedges to squeeze over, and garnish with chives (if using).

Tips + tricks

+ Marinara mix is a combination of mussels, squid, fish and sometimes prawns and is available from most supermarkets. If you can't find it pre-packaged, you could buy the components separately.
+ If you're using frozen prawns or marinara mix, you don't need to defrost them first as they will thaw quickly when added to the soup mixture in the pot.
+ I finely chop the onion, celery and garlic together in my pull chopper so that the pieces are nice and small.

BROCCOLI AND BLUE CHEESE SOUP

Broccoli and blue cheese go so well together. This is a rich, flavoursome soup so it may not be one to make for the kids, but it's ideal as an entree when you are entertaining.

Ready in 1 hour
Serves 6

1 Tbsp butter
1 onion, finely chopped
3 stalks celery, sliced
1 clove garlic, finely diced
2 heads broccoli
2 medium potatoes, peeled and diced
1 litre (35 fl oz) salt-reduced chicken stock
80 g (2¾ oz) blue cheese, crumbled
salt and cracked black pepper, to taste

To serve

20 g (¾ oz) blue cheese, crumbled
cream (optional)

1. Melt the butter in a large pot over a low heat. Add the onion, celery and garlic and sauté for 5–10 minutes until softened.
2. Chop both of the broccoli heads into florets. Trim the outer edges of the stalks then dice the remainder.
3. Set aside 1 cup of broccoli florets. Add the remaining florets, diced stalk, potatoes and stock to the pot. Simmer for 20 minutes until the potato is cooked.
4. Blend the soup in batches in a heat-resistant blender, or use a stick blender. Once smooth, pour the soup back into the pot and bring to a simmer.
5. Roughly chop the reserved broccoli and add to the pot with the blue cheese. Stir through and simmer for a further 5 minutes until the florets are cooked through.
6. Season to taste with salt and pepper, then serve in individual bowls. Sprinkle over the remaining blue cheese and add a drizzle of cream if you desire.

Tips + tricks

+ If you're not a fan of blue cheese, you can substitute tasty cheese. Or leave it out altogether.
+ This soup freezes well. Store in an airtight container in the freezer for up to 3 months. Reheat until piping hot.
+ Take care when blending the soup. Some blenders won't take hot liquids, so if you don't have a heat-resistant blender allow the soup to cool slightly first, or use a stick blender. When removing the blender lid, be careful of any steam.

HEARTY PIES

WHAT'S IN THIS CHAPTER

CHICKEN POT PIE

A tasty chicken pie filling topped with fluffy, rosemary-flavoured scone dumplings . . . this recipe does take some effort, but I assure you, the results are well worth it. This is one of my all-time favourite meals to make when I have a bit of extra time. I highly recommend chopping all your veggies before cooking so that you can easily add them to the pot as you go.

Ready in 1 hour 10 minutes
Serves 6+

Scone Dumplings

2 cups plain flour
2 tsp baking powder
½ tsp salt
1½ Tbsp chopped fresh rosemary
¾ cup milk, plus extra for brushing
50 ml (1¾ fl oz) vegetable oil
½ tsp sea salt

1 Tbsp butter
1 kg (2 lb 4 oz) boneless chicken thighs, diced
2 onions, diced
2 stalks celery, sliced
2 carrots, peeled and sliced
2 cloves garlic, crushed
1 tsp mild curry powder
250 g (9 oz) mushrooms, sliced
1 Tbsp dried mixed herbs
1 tsp salt
½ cup white wine
520 g (1 lb 2 oz) can creamy mushroom soup

1. To make the Scone Dumplings, place all the ingredients except the sea salt in a large bowl and mix to combine. Knead together. Scoop out a heaped tablespoon at a time and roll into small balls (about 18). Place on a plate and chill while you make the pie filling.
2. Preheat the oven to 180°C (350°F) fan bake.
3. Heat the butter in a large cast-iron pot. Brown the chicken in two batches. Remove from the pan and set aside.
4. Add the onions, celery, carrots, garlic and curry powder to the pot. Cook until tender.
5. Add the mushrooms, mixed herbs and salt. Cook, stirring, for 5–10 minutes or until the mushrooms have softened.
6. Deglaze the pan with the wine. Pour in the mushroom soup. Add the cooked chicken and juices back to the pot and stir to combine. Bring to a simmer and cook for 10 minutes until the filling has thickened up slightly. Remove from the heat.
7. Remove the Scone Dumplings from the fridge. Flatten each ball slightly before arranging on top of the pie filling. Brush with a little milk and sprinkle the sea salt on top.
8. Bake for 30–35 minutes or until the scones are golden and cooked through. Remove from the oven and allow to stand for 10 minutes before serving.

Tips + tricks

+ Ensure your pot is large enough to hold all the ingredients. If the scone dumplings are too close to the top, the filling can bubble over.
+ Mashed potato can be used instead of the scone dumplings if you prefer. Or use regular or gluten-free pastry.

PULLED PORK AND APPLE PIE

I think this is one of my all-time favourite pies — I was so proud of how this turned out! You pressure cook the pork (or see tips to slow cook or bake it), make a delicious gravy and then top it with flaky puff pastry. The pork cooks in a sauce made with apples, adding to the beautiful rich flavour.

Ready in 2 hours 20 minutes
Serves 6–8

Pulled Pork

1.5 kg (3 lb 5 oz) pork leg
1 onion, sliced
3 apples, peeled and quartered
1 cup chicken stock
1 Tbsp brown sugar
½ tsp cinnamon
2 Tbsp apple cider vinegar
1 Tbsp mustard
1 Tbsp Worcestershire sauce

50 g (1¾ oz) butter
¼ cup plain flour
salt and cracked black pepper, to season
2 sheets puff pastry
1 egg, beaten

To serve

steamed green vegetables or a side salad

1. To make the Pulled Pork, place all the ingredients in the pressure cooker and put the lid on. Set the cooker to 'Manual' and cook for 1 hour 20 minutes.
2. Once cooked, carefully remove the pork from the pressure cooker and place in a large bowl. Keep the cooking juices in the dish of the cooker to make the gravy later.
3. Preheat the oven to 180°C (350°F) fan bake.
4. Remove any fat and bones from the pork. Shred the pork with 2 forks and set aside.
5. Melt the butter in a shallow casserole dish over a low heat. Sprinkle over the flour and fry off for a few minutes, mixing to combine.
6. Ladle in the reserved cooking juices, a large spoonful at a time, mixing as you go. Once the sauce has thickened up, add the shredded pork. Season well with salt and pepper, and mix to combine. Remove from the heat.
7. Place the puff pastry on top of the casserole dish, trimming the edges to fit. Brush with the egg wash.
8. Bake for 40 minutes until golden brown. Remove from the oven and allow to stand for 10 minutes before serving with steamed greens or a salad.

Tips + tricks

+ To cook the pork in a slow cooker, cook on high for 6+ hours until the meat is falling off the bone and pulls apart easily.
+ To cook the pork in the oven, bake at 160°C (315°F) in a casserole dish with the lid on for 4 hours or until the meat is falling off the bone and pulls apart easily.

BEEF COTTAGE PIES

There's something about a cottage pie that is super-warming and comforting during the cooler months. You can make this in individual servings or as one big pie. The mashed potato topping is also delicious just on its own, and could be served alongside the Beef Short Ribs on page 40 or Pork Chops with Mushroom Sauce on page 28.

Ready in 1 hour
Makes 6 individual pies

Mashed Potatoes

900 g (2 lb) potatoes, peeled and chopped
2 Tbsp butter
½ cup milk
salt and cracked black pepper, to taste

1 Tbsp oil
1 onion, diced
1 large carrot, peeled and diced
500 g (1 lb 2 oz) beef mince
2 cloves garlic, crushed
1 Tbsp dried mixed herbs
⅓ cup red wine (optional)
1 Tbsp wholegrain mustard
2 Tbsp tomato sauce
2 cups beef stock
2 Tbsp cornflour
2 Tbsp water
1 cup peas
salt and cracked black pepper, to taste
1 cup grated cheese

1. Preheat the oven to 180°C (350°F) fan bake.
2. To make the Mashed Potatoes, add the potatoes to a large pot. Cover with water and bring to the boil. Reduce to medium heat and simmer for 15–20 minutes until tender.
3. Drain the potatoes. Mash with the butter and milk and season to taste with salt and pepper. Set aside while you make the filling.
4. Heat the oil in a large frying pan. Add the onion and carrot and fry until softened.
5. Add the mince, garlic and mixed herbs and fry until lightly browned.
6. Stir in the wine (if using), mustard, tomato sauce and stock. Simmer for 10 minutes.
7. Mix the cornflour and water to make a slurry, then add to the frying pan. Add the peas and stir until the filling heats up and thickens. Season to taste with salt and pepper.
8. Divide the pie filling among 6 individual pie dishes and top with Mashed Potatoes, smoothing with the back of a spoon. Sprinkle over the cheese.
9. Bake for 20 minutes or until the cheese is lightly browned with crispy bits.

Tips + tricks

+ This recipe can also be made in one large pie dish.
+ Freeze cooked pie filling (or even cooked individual pies) in airtight containers for up to 3 months.

Kids' fave

BUTTER CHICKEN PIES

Butter chicken is such a popular takeaway dish here in New Zealand. This is another way to serve it, in a flaky puff pastry pie. The chicken breast is pan-fried and then shredded, which makes it nice and tender, and the gravy is full of flavour. Your friends and family will be asking for this meal over and over again!

Ready in 1 hour 20 minutes
Makes 4 individual pies or 1 large pie

500 g (1 lb 2 oz) chicken breasts
1 Tbsp olive oil
salt and cracked black pepper, to season
4 sheets puff pastry
1 egg, beaten

Butter Chicken Gravy

1 onion, finely diced
2 Tbsp butter
1 tsp garam masala
1 tsp ground coriander
1 tsp ground cumin
1 tsp paprika
1 tsp salt
1 tsp cinnamon
1 tsp white sugar
1 Tbsp crushed garlic
1 Tbsp crushed ginger
2 Tbsp tomato paste
2 Tbsp plain flour
1 cup water
½ cup cream

To serve

steamed green vegetables

1. Cut the chicken breasts in half horizontally. Drizzle with the oil and season well with salt and pepper.
2. Heat a large frying pan over a medium-high heat. Cook the chicken for a few minutes on each side, until cooked through. Transfer the chicken to a bowl, cover with tinfoil and set aside to cool.
3. To make the Butter Chicken Gravy, add the onion and half the butter to the same pan. Sauté over a low heat for a few minutes.
4. Add the garam masala, coriander, cumin, paprika, salt, cinnamon and sugar to the pan. Cook off for a few minutes.
5. Add the garlic, ginger and tomato paste to the pan, stirring to combine. Add the remaining butter and allow to melt. Sprinkle over the flour and fry off for a few minutes, mixing as you go.
6. Slowly add in the water, half a cup at a time. Stir to combine. Pour in the cream and cook for a few minutes until nice and thick. Remove from the heat and allow to cool for 10 minutes.
7. Preheat the oven to 180°C (350°F) fan bake. Grease 4 small pie dishes or 1 large pie dish.
8. Shred the chicken breasts. Add the shredded chicken to the sauce with any cooking juices. Stir to combine.
9. Line the pie dish(es) with pastry, trimming the edges as you go. Spoon in the chicken filling, distributing evenly. Place the remaining pastry on top of the pie(s) and seal the edges. Brush with the egg wash.
10. Bake for 40 minutes or until the pastry is golden and flaky. Serve with steamed green veggies on the side.

Kids' fave

LAMB AND SPINACH FILO PIE

This pie was inspired by the beautiful flavours of Mediterranean food, after a holiday to Greece. The spiced lamb goes well with the spinach and ricotta mix and is further complemented by the crunchy filo pastry on top. Although this pie requires a little bit of time and effort to make, it is sure to impress your family and guests.

Ready in 55 minutes
Serves 4–6

Spiced Lamb

1 Tbsp olive oil
1 onion, finely diced
2 cloves garlic, crushed
400 g (14 oz) lamb mince
½ tsp cinnamon
1 tsp ground cumin
1 tsp dried mixed herbs
1 tsp white sugar
1 tsp salt
½ tsp ground black pepper
2 tsp plain flour
400 g (14 oz) can crushed tomatoes

Spinach and Ricotta Layer

300 g (10½ oz) frozen spinach
1 cup grated cheese
250 g (9 oz) ricotta
salt and cracked black pepper, to season

Filo Topping

5 sheets filo pastry
2 Tbsp butter, melted

To serve

fresh salad

1. To make the Spiced Lamb, heat the oil in a large frying pan over a medium heat. Add the onion and garlic and sauté for a few minutes.
2. Add the mince and cook until brown.
3. Add the cinnamon, cumin, mixed herbs, sugar, salt and pepper and cook while stirring. Sprinkle over the flour and stir to combine. Pour in the crushed tomatoes and stir to combine. Remove from the heat.
4. Preheat the oven to 180°C (350°F) fan bake.
5. To make the Spinach and Ricotta Layer, place the spinach in a microwave-proof bowl and microwave for 2 minutes. Transfer to a sieve and squeeze out the excess water.
6. Add the spinach, cheese and ricotta to a large bowl. Season well with salt and pepper and mix to combine.
7. Spoon the Spiced Lamb into the base of a baking dish. Spread out to the edges. Spoon the Spinach and Ricotta over the top and spread out to the edges.
8. To make the Filo Topping, brush a sheet of filo with melted butter and scrunch softly. Place on top of the pie filling. Repeat with the remaining filo until the filling is completely covered.
9. Bake for 25 minutes until golden and crispy.
10. Serve immediately alongside a fresh salad.

Tips + tricks

+ This is a great recipe to double for a dinner party.

MINCE AND CHEESE PIE

I had to include a mince and cheese pie in this cookbook. This one has the classic Kiwi bakery-style flavour from my childhood. So nostalgic! You can make this as one big family pie like I have here, or as smaller individual pies if you prefer.

Ready in 1 hour 10 minutes
Serves 4–6

1 Tbsp oil, for frying
1 onion, finely chopped
2 cloves garlic, crushed
500 g (1 lb 2 oz) beef mince
2 Tbsp plain flour
1 Tbsp tomato paste
1 Tbsp Worcestershire sauce
1 tsp dried mixed herbs
2 cups beef stock
salt and cracked black pepper, to taste
2 sheets flaky puff pastry
1 cup grated cheese
1 egg, whisked

To serve

mashed potatoes
cooked peas
tomato sauce

1. Preheat the oven to 190°C (375°F) fan bake. Grease a 20 cm (8 in) square pie dish.
2. Heat the oil in a large frying pan over a low heat. Add the onion and sauté for a few minutes.
3. Add the garlic and stir to combine. Increase the heat and add the beef mince. Cook until browned, breaking the mince up as you go.
4. Sprinkle over the flour, and fry off for 2 minutes.
5. Stir in the tomato paste, Worcestershire sauce and mixed herbs. Pour in the stock and mix to combine. Reduce the heat and simmer for 5 minutes until the liquid has reduced.
6. Season to taste with salt and pepper. Set aside to cool.
7. Line the prepared pie dish with a sheet of pastry. Add the cooled filling and sprinkle over the cheese. Place the remaining pastry on top and seal the edges. Brush with the egg wash.
8. Bake for 40 minutes until golden brown.
9. Remove from the oven and allow to stand for 10 minutes before serving.
10. Serve alongside mashed potatoes and peas, with your favourite tomato sauce.

Tips + tricks

+ Frozen mixed veggies could be added to the mince filling to bulk it up.

Kids' fave

BACON AND EGG PIE

Another classic I had to include in this book. If you haven't tried a bacon and egg pie with the addition of caramelised red onions and tomato relish, you are in for a treat. Slices are perfect for a filling snack on-the-go or a shared picnic — or, for a complete meal, serve this alongside a fresh green salad. As with all the recipes in this chapter, feel free to make individual pies instead of a large one if you prefer.

Ready in 1 hour 20 minutes
Serves 6

1 Tbsp olive oil
2 red onions, finely sliced
2 Tbsp finely chopped fresh Italian parsley
12 eggs
salt and cracked black pepper, to season
3 sheets puff pastry
250 g (9 oz) bacon rashers, chopped
¼ cup tomato relish or chutney

1. Preheat the oven to 180°C (350°F) fan bake.
2. Add the oil to a frying pan over a medium heat. Add the red onions and sauté for 5–10 minutes until soft.
3. Whisk together the parsley and 6 eggs in a large bowl. Season well with salt and pepper.
4. Line the base and sides of a 32 × 20 cm (12½ × 8 in) baking dish with pastry. Pour in the egg mixture, leaving a little egg residue in the bowl for brushing the pastry later. Scatter in the bacon and cooked red onion.
5. Crack the remaining eggs directly on top, using a fork to break the yolks if desired. Add dollops of relish or chutney and season again with salt and pepper.
6. Place the remaining pastry on top of the pie and seal the edges. Brush with the leftover egg mixture from the bowl.
7. Bake for 50 minutes until golden and cooked through.
8. Remove from the oven and allow to stand for 10 minutes before serving.

Tips + tricks

+ This pie can be enjoyed warm or cold the next day. It also freezes really well in portions for a quick and easy lunch.
+ If you do not like whole eggs in your pie you can whisk all 12 together.
+ You can leave the relish or chutney out and serve it on the side if you prefer.

SLOW-COOKER FAVOURITES

WHAT'S IN THIS CHAPTER

EASY BEEF CURRY

I love how tender the beef comes out in this recipe. The coconut cream gives it a lovely flavour, and the addition of the beans at the end gives it some colour and crunch.

Ready in 4 hours 10 minutes
Serves 8

Curry Sauce
2 cups beef stock
400 ml (14 fl oz) can coconut cream
400 g (14 oz) can crushed tomatoes
4 Tbsp yellow curry paste
2 Tbsp crushed garlic
2 Tbsp garam masala
2 tsp brown sugar
2 tsp crushed ginger

1.2 kg (2 lb 10 oz) diced beef
2 carrots, peeled and sliced
1 onion, sliced
2 Tbsp cornflour
2 Tbsp water
100 g (3½ oz) green beans, trimmed and chopped

To serve
steamed white rice
chopped fresh Italian parsley or coriander
steamed green vegetables

1. To make the Curry Sauce, add all the ingredients to a large jug. Mix to combine.
2. Add the beef, carrots and onion to a slow cooker.
3. Pour the Curry Sauce over the beef and vegetables. Mix to combine.
4. Cook on high for 3 hours 45 minutes.
5. Mix together the cornflour and water, and stir into the slow cooker with the green beans. Cook on high for a further 15 minutes.
6. Serve on top of steamed rice with a garnish of fresh herbs and steamed greens on the side.

Tips + tricks

+ This recipe makes a large quantity, so you can save half for later if you like. Freeze in airtight containers for up to 3 months.
+ You can cook this in the oven if you don't have a slow cooker. Place the ingredients in an ovenproof dish and bake at 180°C (350°F) for 60–80 minutes or until the beef is falling apart.

CREAMY SHREDDED CHICKEN

I can't believe how popular this recipe is on the website. The beauty of this dish is that you throw it all in the slow cooker with the cream cheese, then mix and shred the chicken at the end. It's perfect served on fresh buns, on pizzas or in wraps.

Ready in 4 hours 10 minutes
Serves 6

½ × 400 g (14 oz) can crushed tomatoes
2 Tbsp chipotle sauce (optional)
2 tsp brown sugar
1 Tbsp dried mixed herbs
1 tsp salt
1 kg (2 lb 4 oz) chicken breasts
250 g (9 oz) cream cheese

To serve
fresh toasted buns
pre-made coleslaw
spring onion, finely sliced
cheese slices

1. Add the crushed tomatoes, chipotle sauce (if using), sugar, mixed herbs and salt to a slow cooker. Mix to combine. Add the chicken breasts and coat in the sauce.
2. Scoop or cut the cream cheese into chunks and add to the slow cooker, making sure the cream cheese doesn't touch the sides.
3. Cook on high for 4+ hours, or on low for 7+ hours, until the chicken is cooked through and can be shredded easily.
4. Shred the chicken in the slow cooker with 2 forks. Mix the sauce through the shredded chicken.
5. Serve in the buns with coleslaw, spring onion and cheese.

Tips + tricks

+ I like to spray my slow cooker with cooking spray before adding the ingredients. This makes it easier to clean at the end.
+ I used chipotle sauce but you can use your favourite hot sauce or barbecue sauce. Or leave it out if you don't want any spice.
+ Freeze any leftover shredded chicken in sealable bags or an airtight container for up to 3 months.

Kids' fave

VEGETARIAN BEAN CHILLI

I like to make chilli on the stovetop as well, but I wanted to include this easy recipe where you throw everything in the slow cooker and let the flavours come together all day long. I love how versatile this chilli is. I usually serve it on top of freshly steamed rice, but it can also be used on top of nachos or in wraps.

Ready in 4 hours 20 minutes
Serves 12

1 onion
2 carrots, peeled
2 capsicums
3 cloves garlic, crushed
2 tsp smoked paprika
2 tsp ground cumin
1 tsp ground coriander
½ tsp chilli flakes
½ tsp chipotle powder (optional)
1 tsp brown sugar
1 tsp salt
1 vegetable stock cube
2 × 400 g (14 oz) cans crushed tomatoes
2 × 400 g (14 oz) cans red kidney beans
2 × 400 g (14 oz) cans black beans

To serve
steamed rice
corn chips
sour cream
grated cheese
chopped fresh coriander

1. Finely chop the onion, carrots and capsicums, then place in the base of a slow cooker. Add the garlic, paprika, cumin, coriander, chilli flakes, chipotle powder (if using), sugar and salt.
2. Crush the stock cube in the packet. Add to the slow cooker with the crushed tomatoes.
3. Using a sieve, drain and rinse the kidney beans and black beans. Add to the slow cooker and stir to combine all the ingredients.
4. Cook on low for 8 hours or on high for 4 hours.
5. Serve on top of steamed rice with sour cream, grated cheese and coriander.

Tips + tricks

+ This recipe makes a large quantity, so you can save half for later if you like. Freeze in airtight containers for up to 3 months.

WARM

Falcon

SMOKY SAUSAGE CASSEROLE

I am always looking for new ideas for sausages. This casserole is great because the potatoes cook in the slow cooker with the sausages and the other ingredients, so they take on all of the flavour. I like to brown the sausages first, but you don't have to do that if you are short on time.

Ready in 3 hours 30 minutes
Serves 4

8 sausages
1 Tbsp olive oil
1 onion, finely sliced
3 cloves garlic, crushed
1 Tbsp brown sugar
2 Tbsp plain flour
400 g (14 oz) can red kidney beans, drained
1 tsp ground cumin
1 tsp smoked paprika
2 Tbsp Worcestershire sauce
1 beef stock cube
2 cups boiling water
4 medium potatoes
salt and cracked black pepper, to taste

To serve
steamed green vegetables
butter
sour cream

1. Brown the sausages on each side in a dry frying pan. Transfer the browned sausages to a slow cooker.
2. Add the oil to the same pan and sauté the onion for a few minutes, until turning soft.
3. Add the garlic and heat through for 1 minute. Stir in the sugar. Add the flour and mix together, using a spoon to get all of the bits off the frying pan.
4. Transfer the onion mixture to the slow cooker. Add the kidney beans, cumin, paprika and Worcestershire sauce. Dissolve the stock cube in the boiling water, then pour into the slow cooker. Stir everything together. Place the potatoes on top.
5. Cook on high for 3–4 hours until the potatoes are cooked through and the casserole is nice and thick. You may have to stir the mixture halfway through the cook time and turn the potatoes over.
6. Season to taste with salt and pepper. Serve the sausages with a large spoonful of hot smoky bean sauce and greens on the side. Add the potatoes with butter and a dollop of sour cream on top.

Tips + tricks

+ This could be made in a cast-iron dish in the oven. Just bake for 1.5–2 hours at 180°C (350°F) fan bake until the potatoes are cooked through. Remove the lid for the last 15 minutes to thicken up the sauce.

SPAGHETTI BOLOGNESE

I had to make sure I included a recipe for slow-cooker spaghetti bolognese. It is essential that you brown the onion and mince before adding them to the slow cooker as this will add lots of flavour. The cool thing about this meal is you can blend up some spinach with the tomatoes to hide the veggies from the kids. I like to grate the carrots and finely dice the onion, too.

Ready in 4 hours 15 minutes
Serves 10

1 Tbsp oil
800 g (1 lb 12 oz) beef mince
1 onion, grated or finely diced
70 g (2½ oz) baby spinach (optional)
2 × 400 g (14 oz) cans chopped tomatoes
2 carrots, grated
3 cloves garlic, crushed
2 tsp dried Italian herbs
½ tsp white sugar
2 Tbsp tomato paste
1 cup beef stock (I use a stock cube and boiling water)
salt and cracked black pepper, to season

To serve
500 g (1 lb 2 oz) spaghetti, cooked
parmesan

1. Place a large frying pan over a medium heat and add the oil. Add the mince and onion and cook until the mince has browned. Transfer to a slow cooker.
2. Blend the spinach (if using) and half the tomatoes in a blender until finely chopped.
3. Add the carrots, garlic, Italian herbs, sugar, tomato paste, stock, spinach mix and remaining tomatoes to the slow cooker. Season well with salt and pepper and stir together.
4. Cook on high for 4 hours or on low for 6+ hours.
5. Stir everything together at the end. Check the seasoning and add more if needed.
6. Arrange the cooked spaghetti in the bottom of a large bowl and place the bolognese on top. Grate over the parmesan and serve immediately.

Tips + tricks

+ This recipe makes a large quantity, so you can save half for later if you like. Freeze in airtight containers for up to 3 months.
+ The bolognese mixture is also great for lasagne and other Italian-style mince dishes.
+ Add extra vegetables, like chopped mushrooms or capsicums, at the same time as the carrots if you like.

Kids' fave

LAMB SHANKS

This was one of the first slow-cooker recipes on my website years ago and it has been super-popular ever since. It is very simple to make and great for when you can get lamb shanks on special.

Ready in 4 hours 15 minutes
Serves 4

4 lamb shanks
1 large onion, sliced
2 carrots, peeled and chopped
400 g (14 oz) can crushed tomatoes
2 cups beef stock
1 Tbsp ground cumin
1 tsp salt
3 bay leaves
1 Tbsp cornflour

To serve
mashed potatoes
steamed green vegetables
chopped fresh Italian parsley

1. Cut into the lamb shanks around the bone end so that the meat bunches up while cooking.
2. Add the lamb shanks, onion, carrots, crushed tomatoes, stock, cumin, salt and bay leaves to a slow cooker and mix to combine. Make sure the bones are sticking up and put the lid on.
3. Cook on high for 4 hours or on low for up to 8 hours. Mix the cornflour with a little cold water and pour in for the last 20 minutes of cook time to thicken up the liquid.
4. Serve the lamb shanks and sauce on mashed potatoes, with steamed greens on the side. Garnish with the parsley.

Tips + tricks

+ This recipe could also be made in a cast-iron dish in the oven. Bake covered for 2–3 hours at 160°C (315°F) fan bake until the meat is falling off the bone.
+ Leftover lamb shank meat and gravy is delicious stirred through cooked pappardelle pasta.

BARBECUE BEEF BRISKET WITH SMASHED POTATOES

Sometimes it's hard to get beef brisket right, but this is a great way to get it nice and tender. You slow cook it all day and then to get the lovely glaze around the outside, you pop it under the grill at the end of the cooking. The potatoes cook in the slow cooker with the meat, and then you put them in the oven to make them nice and crispy.

Ready in 7 hours + marinating time
Serves 6+

Spice Rub
2 tsp brown sugar
2 tsp paprika
2 tsp garlic powder
2 tsp ground cumin
2 tsp flaky sea salt
2 tsp dried mixed herbs
½ tsp cracked black pepper

2–3 kg (4 lb 8 oz–6 lb 12 oz) beef brisket
¼ cup water
2 Tbsp HP sauce
1 cup barbecue sauce
6 medium potatoes
1 Tbsp olive oil
flaky sea salt
1 Tbsp cornflour
2 Tbsp cold water

To serve
cooked peas
butter
sour cream

1. To make the Spice Rub, mix together all the ingredients.
2. Trim excess fat off the brisket, and rub all over with the Spice Rub. If you have time, marinate for 2 hours or overnight.
3. Add the water, HP sauce and ½ cup of the barbecue sauce to the base of a slow cooker and mix together. Place the brisket on top.
4. Cook on high for 3–4 hours. Turn over the brisket and add the potatoes. Cook on high for a further 2 hours.
5. Preheat the oven to 210°C (410°F) fan grill. Line a tray with baking paper.
6. Place the brisket on the prepared tray. Arrange the potatoes around the brisket. Brush ¼ cup of the barbecue sauce over the top of the brisket. Use a potato masher to crush the potatoes. Drizzle each potato with the oil and season with flaky sea salt.
7. Place in the oven under the grill (but not too close). Bake for 20 minutes until the top caramelises and the potatoes are crisp and golden.
8. Pour the liquid from the slow cooker into a pot over a medium heat. Skim off and discard any fat that floats to the top. Stir in the remaining ¼ cup of barbecue sauce. Bring to a simmer and reduce the gravy for 10 minutes.

Continued overleaf . . .

9. Mix the cornflour and cold water, then stir into the pot. Simmer for a few more minutes until the gravy thickens up.
10. Remove the brisket from the oven, cover with tinfoil and set aside to rest for 10 minutes.
11. Thinly slice the brisket across the grain. Serve with the peas, barbecue gravy and potatoes topped with butter and sour cream.

Tips + tricks

+ You could finish this brisket on the barbecue instead of the oven to give it a smoky flavour.
+ Leftover brisket is great served in sandwiches the next day.
+ To cook the brisket in the oven instead of the slow cooker, bake in a covered dish at 160°C (315°F) fan bake for 3 hours. Remove the lid, top the brisket with ¼ cup of barbecue sauce and grill for 20 minutes until the top caramelises.

HONEY SOY CHICKEN

This tasty recipe makes a big batch, so you can freeze half for later if you like. I love feeling organised and having things in the freezer for an easy, ready-to-go meal.

Ready in 3 hours 10 minutes
Serves 8

Honey Soy Marinade
½ cup low-salt soy sauce
1 chicken stock cube dissolved in 1 cup boiling water
2 Tbsp crushed garlic
2 Tbsp crushed ginger
4 Tbsp oyster sauce
6 Tbsp honey

1 kg (2 lb 4 oz) boneless chicken thighs
2 Tbsp cornflour
2 Tbsp water

To serve
steamed white rice
spring onion, finely sliced
sesame seeds
steamed green vegetables

1. To make the Honey Soy Marinade, add all the ingredients to a jug and mix to combine.
2. Cut each chicken thigh into 3 pieces and add to the slow cooker.
3. Pour the Honey Soy Marinade over the chicken. Stir to coat.
4. Cook on high for 2 hours 45 minutes.
5. Mix together the cornflour and water and stir into the slow cooker. Cook on high for a further 15 minutes.
6. Shred the chicken in the slow cooker with 2 forks.
7. Serve on top of steamed rice with spring onion and sesame seeds scattered over and steamed greens on the side.

Tips + tricks

+ You can cook this in the oven if you don't have a slow cooker. Place the ingredients in an ovenproof dish and bake covered at 180°C (350°F) for 1 hour or until the chicken is cooked through.
+ If you love this recipe, you can multiply the ingredients and cook a larger portion for a crowd.
+ Freeze any leftover honey soy chicken in sealable bags or an airtight container for up to 3 months.

Kids' fave

MEXICAN PULLED BEEF

This pulled beef is packed with flavour and is so versatile. I love it on tacos, burritos, enchiladas, quesadillas, baked potatoes, nachos, burgers, pizza, wedges or rice.

Ready in 5 hours 10 minutes
Serves 8

Mexican Sauce
400 g (14 oz) can crushed tomatoes
1 Tbsp paprika
1 Tbsp cumin
1 Tbsp cornflour
2 Tbsp sweet chilli sauce
1 tsp salt
1 beef stock cube, crushed
2 cloves garlic, crushed
1 onion, sliced
½ cup boiling water

1 kg (2 lb 4 oz) beef chuck steak, casserole beef, beef cheeks or brisket pieces

1. To make the Mexican Sauce, add all the ingredients to the base of a slow cooker and mix to combine.
2. Cut the beef into large chunks and add to the slow cooker. Stir to coat in the sauce.
3. Cook on high for 5+ hours or on low for 8+ hours.
4. Once the beef is falling apart easily, use forks to shred apart any large pieces. Stir through the sauce. Turn the slow cooker on to the warm function until ready to serve.

Tips + tricks

+ Freeze any leftover beef in sealable bags or airtight containers for up to 3 months.
+ If you want to serve this with baked potatoes, add whole potatoes on top of the beef in the slow cooker for the last 2 hours of the cook time.
+ This recipe is mild so add some chilli flakes or hot sauce to spice it up if you like.

BAKING & SWEET TREATS

WHAT'S IN THIS CHAPTER

Snickerdoodles p160

Carrot Cake p162

Mashed Potato Bread p164

No-bake Lemon Slice p168

Brioche Loaf p170

Raw Chocolate Slice p174

Tan Slice p176

BANANA BREAD

We all need a great banana bread recipe up our sleeves. This one is so easy and makes a great loaf that isn't too sweet. I love to have my banana bread toasted for breakfast the next day and, as always, I serve it with a generous spread of butter.

Ready in 1 hour 15 minutes
Makes 1 medium loaf

3 ripe bananas
110 g (3¾ oz) butter, melted
1 egg
¾ cup white sugar
1 tsp vanilla essence
1⅔ cups plain flour
1 tsp baking soda
½ tsp salt

To serve
butter

1. Preheat the oven to 170°C (325°F) fan bake. Line a 24 × 13 cm (9½ × 5 in) loaf tin with baking paper.
2. Add the bananas to a large bowl and mash with a fork.
3. Add the melted butter, egg, sugar and vanilla to the bowl. Mix to combine.
4. Sift the flour, baking soda and salt into the bowl. Gently fold together.
5. Pour the mixture into the prepared tin and spread it out to the edges.
6. Bake for 50–60 minutes until golden and a skewer inserted into the centre comes out clean.
7. Slice and serve with butter.
8. Store in an airtight container in the pantry for up to 4 days, or in the fridge for up to a week. This loaf can also be frozen for up to 6 months if wrapped tightly in cling film.

Tips + tricks

+ If you're using frozen bananas, you can microwave them to room temperature.
+ The number of bananas in the recipe is flexible, as long as you end up with at least 1 cup once mashed.
+ I like to double this recipe and make a loaf for the freezer.

PANCAKES

A classic pancake recipe is essential for a home cook. For this one I use a quarter-cup measure to pour the batter into the pan, and the pancakes come out the perfect size every time. These are just like McDonald's hotcakes! I like to stack these up and let everyone serve themselves.

Ready in 25 minutes
Makes 12 pancakes

50 g (1¾ oz) butter, plus extra for frying
1¼ cups milk
1 egg
1½ cups plain flour
1 Tbsp baking powder
3 Tbsp white sugar
¼ tsp salt

To serve
maple syrup, butter or toppings of your choice

1. Add the butter to a large glass bowl and microwave for 30 seconds. Add the milk and microwave for a further 30 seconds. Whisk together.
2. Crack in the egg and whisk to combine. Sift in the flour and baking powder. Add the sugar and salt. Whisk together until the batter is smooth with no lumps.
3. Heat a large frying pan to a medium heat and add a little butter. Scoop ¼ cup of batter for each pancake into the frying pan and cook until bubbles form on top. Flip over and cook until golden on the other side.
4. Keep the pancakes warm in the oven while you make the rest of the batch.
5. Serve warm with the toppings of your choice.

Tips + tricks

+ If you want larger pancakes then use ½ cup of batter for each one and cook one at a time in the frying pan.
+ Other toppings could include ice cream, fruit compote, natural yoghurt, banana or bacon.
+ You can make the batter the night before if desired — just give it a quick whisk while the frying pan is heating up.

Kids' fave

HOME-MADE MUESLI

I love to make a big batch of this toasted muesli and keep it in a container in the pantry. It lasts for a few weeks and makes for a quick and tasty breakfast. It's versatile, too, so add whichever nuts, seeds and dried fruit you prefer. This is delicious served with your favourite yoghurt and fruit or fruit compote.

Ready in 45 minutes
Serves 16

4 cups wholegrain oats
2 cups rolled oats
1 cup cashews
¾ cup sunflower seeds
¼ cup pumpkin seeds
1 cup shredded coconut
2 tsp cinnamon
4 Tbsp coconut oil
4 Tbsp rice bran oil
4 Tbsp maple syrup
4 Tbsp honey
1 cup dried apricots, chopped (optional)

1. Preheat the oven to 160°C (315°F) fan bake.
2. Add the oats, cashews, sunflower seeds, pumpkin seeds, coconut and cinnamon to a large roasting dish. Mix to combine.
3. Place the oils, maple syrup and honey in a glass jug. Melt in the microwave in 30-second bursts until the coconut oil has melted. Mix to combine. Pour over the dry ingredients and mix everything together with a spatula.
4. Bake for 30 minutes, stirring every 10 minutes.
5. Remove from the oven and add the chopped apricots (if using). Set aside to cool.
6. Once cooled, store in an airtight container in the pantry for up to 4 weeks.

muesli

BLENDER WAFFLES

The best thing about this recipe is that all the ingredients get mixed together in the blender so you can conveniently pour the batter straight into the waffle iron. Everyone who has tried this swears by it. Waffles are great for breakfast or even dessert, with some vanilla ice cream and the toppings of your choice.

Ready in 15 minutes
Makes 10 waffles

1½ cups milk
1 tsp vanilla essence or extract
3 eggs
60 g (2¼ oz) butter, melted and cooled
2 cups self-raising flour
¼ cup caster sugar

To serve
whipped cream, berry compote, chocolate sauce or toppings of your choice

1. Add the milk, vanilla, eggs and melted butter to a blender and blend until well combined.
2. Add the flour and sugar, then blend again. Use a spatula to scrape any flour off the sides and blend until the batter is smooth with no lumps.
3. Heat the waffle iron and pour in the batter as directed. Keep the cooked waffles in a warm oven until all of the batter is used up.
4. Serve warm, with the toppings of your choice.

Tips + tricks

+ The batter can be made the night before and stored in the fridge to use the next day.
+ Extra cooked waffles can be stored in an airtight container or sealable bag in the fridge for up to 3 days, or in the freezer for up to 4 weeks. Reheat in the microwave or toaster.

Kids' fave

H

DATE AND ORANGE SCONES

A scone is such a lovely treat for morning tea, and these ones have a beautiful aroma with the addition of the orange juice and zest. Enjoy these warm with a generous amount of butter and a cup of tea.

Ready in 30 minutes
Makes 9 scones

3 cups plain flour
4 tsp baking powder
½ tsp salt
3 Tbsp white sugar
½ tsp mixed spice
90 g (3¼ oz) cold butter, cubed
1 orange
about ¾ cup milk, plus extra for brushing
1½ cups chopped dates

To serve
butter

1. Preheat the oven to 220°C (425°F) fan bake. Line a baking tray with baking paper.
2. Add the flour, baking powder, salt, sugar, mixed spice and butter to a food processor. Blitz until the butter is incorporated and the mix resembles breadcrumbs. To achieve this without a food processor, rub the butter into the flour using your fingertips.
3. Pour the flour mixture into a large mixing bowl and create a well in the centre.
4. Zest and juice the orange into a measuring jug, then top up with enough milk so you have 1 cup of liquid.
5. Add the orange and milk mixture to the flour mixture. Stir with a knife until almost combined. Add the dates and finish mixing.
6. Place the dough on a floured surface and roll out into a square. Cut into 9 squares.
7. Transfer the scones to the prepared tray and brush the tops with milk.
8. Bake for 10–12 minutes or until golden brown.
9. Transfer to a rack to cool slightly, then serve warm with butter.

Tips + tricks

+ Overmixing will create tough and more dense scones. To ensure yours are fluffy and soft, mix just enough to incorporate the wet and dry ingredients, then stop.

KRISPIE BISCUIT CAKE

This cake is so moreish, you simply can't stop eating it. Krispie biscuits are plain New Zealand biscuits made with coconut, but you could use whatever plain biscuits you have in the pantry. This can also be made in a large slice tin if you prefer.

Ready in 25 minutes + setting time
Makes 1 cake

250 g (9 oz) butter
250 g (9 oz) white sugar
2 tsp vanilla essence
4 Tbsp cocoa powder
2 eggs
2 × 225 g (8 oz) packets Krispie biscuits, roughly crushed

Chocolate Icing

1 cup icing sugar
2 Tbsp cocoa powder
1 Tbsp butter, softened
2 Tbsp boiling water

1. Line a 22 cm (8½ in) round springform cake tin with baking paper.
2. Add the butter to a large pot and melt. Add the sugar and bring to a simmer. Remove from the heat and add the vanilla and cocoa. Mix to combine.
3. Add the eggs while the mixture is still hot and whisk thoroughly until glossy and combined. Pour in the crushed biscuits and mix to coat in the mixture.
4. Press into the prepared tin and spread to the edges with the back of a spoon.
5. To make the Chocolate Icing, whisk together all the ingredients until smooth. Spread over the cake in the tin. Chill for at least 4 hours or overnight until set.
6. Remove from the tin, slice into pieces and serve. Store in an airtight container in the fridge for up to a week.

Tips + tricks

+ You can use a food processor or rolling pin to crush the biscuits, but don't crush them too finely as you want some chunky bits.
+ Swap the Krispie biscuits for Super Wines, Milk Arrowroots, Maries or another plain biscuit of your choice.

PALLARES
SOLSONA

ANZAC BISCUITS

I've always been a bit cheeky and made my Anzac biscuits with chocolate drops in them. But if you are a traditionalist, you can easily make these without the chocolate. So many of my readers say these are their ultimate favourite Anzac biscuits.

Ready in 40 minutes + chilling time
Makes 16 cookies

1 cup rolled oats
1 cup desiccated coconut
1 cup brown sugar
1 cup plain flour
125 g (4½ oz) butter
2 Tbsp golden syrup
1 tsp baking soda
2 Tbsp boiling water
1 cup chocolate drops

1. Mix together the oats, coconut, sugar and flour in a large bowl.
2. Add the butter and golden syrup to a jug and melt together in the microwave for 30 seconds.
3. Dissolve the baking soda in the boiling water. Add to the butter mixture and stir.
4. Add the butter mixture to the dry ingredients and stir to combine. Pour in the chocolate drops and stir together. Chill for 30 minutes.
5. Preheat the oven to 160°C (315°F) fan bake. Line 2 baking trays with baking paper.
6. Roll the chilled mixture into balls and place on the prepared trays. I use a heaped tablespoon of mixture for each ball, but you can make them any size you like.
7. Bake for 15–20 minutes until golden.
8. Cool on the trays for a few minutes, then transfer to a wire rack to cool completely.
9. Store in an airtight container in the pantry for up to 2 weeks.

Tips + tricks

+ You can swap out the chocolate drops for white or dark chocolate chips or buttons.

Kids' fave

JAFFA CAKE

This orange, almond and chocolate cake is perfect for your gluten-free friends and family. You can serve it with or without the dark chocolate ganache on top. I like to have mine with some Greek yoghurt on the side.

Ready in 1 hour 10 minutes
Makes 1 cake

150 g (5½ oz) butter, softened
1 cup white sugar
zest of 3 oranges, plus extra for garnish
4 eggs
200 g (7 oz) ground almonds
½ cup cornflour
2 tsp baking powder

Orange Syrup

200 ml (7 fl oz) orange juice (juice of about 3 oranges)
½ cup icing sugar

Dark Chocolate Ganache

75 ml (2½ fl oz) cream
75 g (2½ oz) dark chocolate, chopped
1 tsp honey

To serve

orange zest or peel

Tips + tricks

+ If you are making this for someone who can't eat gluten, make sure you check the labels of any processed foods to ensure the ingredients are completely gluten-free.

1. Preheat the oven to 160°C (315°F) fan bake. Line a 22 cm (8½ in) round cake tin with baking paper.
2. Add the butter and sugar to the bowl of a stand mixer and cream until light and fluffy.
3. Add the orange zest and mix to combine. Add the eggs, one at a time, mixing on medium speed. Add half the ground almonds and mix until combined. Add the remaining ground almonds, cornflour and baking powder. Mix on low speed until just combined.
4. Spread the cake batter evenly into the prepared tin.
5. Bake for 35–45 minutes or until a skewer inserted into the centre comes out clean.
6. While the cake is baking, make the Orange Syrup. Add the orange juice and icing sugar to a small pot. Simmer, stirring, for 5–10 minutes until thickened and reduced. Set aside.
7. Once the cake is cooked and still in the tin, poke about 15 holes in the top with a chopstick or skewer. Pour over the Orange Syrup until it covers the entire surface. You may have to tilt the tin to get even coverage. Leave the cake in the tin to absorb the syrup and cool completely.
8. To make the Dark Chocolate Ganache, gently heat the cream in a small pot or in the microwave until hot. Add the dark chocolate and honey and allow to sit until the chocolate has melted. Whisk together. Set aside to cool and thicken.
9. Carefully remove the cake from the tin and place on a cake plate. Pour over the cooled ganache and garnish with orange zest or peel. Set aside to allow the ganache to set.
10. Cut into slices and serve.
11. Store in an airtight container in the pantry for up to 5 days.

BAKED APRICOT SLICE

My sister Gemma has been begging me for years to create an apricot slice that is just like one you would buy from a bakery. I love the taste of tart apricots in baking, and the best thing about this recipe is that it uses canned apricots. This makes the slice affordable and means you can enjoy it at any time of the year.

Ready in 50 minutes + setting time
Makes 12 pieces

150 g (5½ oz) butter, softened
1 cup white sugar
1 egg
1 tsp vanilla essence
2 cups plain flour
1 tsp baking powder
1 Tbsp icing sugar (optional)

Apricot Filling

2 × 410 g (14½ oz) cans apricots
¼ cup white sugar
1 Tbsp cornflour

1. Preheat the oven to 170°C (325°F) fan bake. Line a 27 × 17 cm (10¾ × 6½ in) slice tin with baking paper.
2. To make the base, add the butter and sugar to the bowl of a stand mixer and whisk on high until starting to turn pale. Add the egg and vanilla and whisk on high until light and fluffy. Add the flour and baking powder and mix on low until combined.
3. Remove a third of the mixture and set aside for the topping. Add the remaining mixture to the prepared tin, using the back of a metal spoon to push it down and smooth it out to the edges. Use a fork to pierce holes in the top.
4. Bake for 12 minutes. Remove from the oven and set aside.
5. While the base is baking, make the Apricot Filling. Drain the cans of apricots, reserving the juice. Chop the apricots into small pieces on a large chopping board. Add the chopped apricots, ⅓ cup of the reserved juice, sugar and cornflour to a small pot and stir to combine. Simmer, while stirring, for 15 minutes until the sauce has reduced.
6. Use a potato masher to break up any large pieces of apricot. Pour the Apricot Filling over the cooked base, then scatter chunks of the reserved base mixture over the top.
7. Bake for a further 25 minutes.
8. Remove from the oven and allow to cool in the tin.
9. Once cooled to room temperature, transfer the slice to the fridge to chill.
10. Once chilled, sift over the icing sugar (if using) and cut into squares. Store in an airtight container in the fridge for up to 5 days.

SNICKERDOODLES

Snickerdoodles are an all-time favourite in our family. My mum, Margot, used to make them back in the '90s and they never lasted longer than a day or two. It's so special to have her recipe here in the cookbook.

Ready in 40 minutes + chilling time
Makes 50 cookies

225 g (8 oz) butter, softened
1¾ cups white sugar
2 eggs
¼ cup milk
1 tsp vanilla essence
3 cups plain flour
½ tsp salt
½ tsp cream of tartar
½ tsp baking soda

Cinnamon-sugar Coating
2 Tbsp cinnamon
⅓ cup white sugar

1. Add the butter and sugar to a stand mixer and cream until fluffy.
2. Add the eggs, milk and vanilla. Mix again until well combined. Sift in the flour, salt, cream of tartar and baking soda and mix on low until just combined.
3. Place the mixing bowl in the fridge for 20 minutes to firm up the dough.
4. Preheat the oven to 180°C (350°F) fan bake. Line 3 baking trays with baking paper.
5. To make the Cinnamon-sugar Coating, mix together the cinnamon and sugar.
6. Roll the cookie dough into small balls (roughly tablespoon size) and coat each one in Cinnamon-sugar Coating.
7. Place on the prepared trays about 5 cm (2 in) apart. Flatten the dough balls to about 1 cm (½ in) thick with the bottom of a glass.
8. Bake for 12 minutes until starting to crisp on the outside but still soft in the centre.
9. Cool on the trays for 10 minutes, then use a spatula to transfer the cookies to baking racks to cool completely.
10. Store in an airtight container in the pantry for up to a week.

Tips + tricks

+ This recipe makes a big batch, so if desired you can freeze balls of uncooked cookie dough in a sealable bag for up to 3 months.

Kids' fave

CARROT CAKE

This is one of the first recipes that my sister Grace (who is an amazing baker) made for the VJ Cooks website and it's been super-popular ever since. Readers say it's the best carrot cake they've ever made. The cream cheese icing is so delicious. Thanks Gracie, you are the best!

Ready in 1 hour 20 minutes
Serves 12

1⅓ cups brown sugar
3 eggs
1 cup neutral oil
1 tsp vanilla essence
1 tsp salt
¼ cup milk
2 cups plain flour
1 tsp baking powder
1 tsp baking soda
1 tsp ground ginger
2 tsp cinnamon
½ tsp ground nutmeg
1 tsp mixed spice
227 g (8 oz) can crushed pineapple, drained
350 g (12 oz) grated carrot (about 3 carrots)

Cream Cheese Icing

60 g (2¼ oz) butter, softened
200 g (7 oz) cream cheese, softened
1 tsp vanilla essence
1 tsp lemon zest
2 cups icing sugar

1. Preheat the oven to 160°C (315°F) fan bake. Line a 22 cm (8½ in) round cake tin with baking paper.
2. Mix together the sugar and eggs in a large bowl. Add the oil, vanilla, salt and milk and whisk together.
3. Sift in the flour, baking powder, baking soda, ginger, cinnamon, nutmeg and mixed spice and mix well.
4. Add the pineapple and carrot to the bowl and combine. Pour into the prepared tin.
5. Bake for 45–55 minutes or until a skewer inserted into the centre comes out clean.
6. Set aside to cool in the tin for 5 minutes, then transfer to a baking rack to cool completely.
7. To make the Cream Cheese Icing, cream the butter in a stand mixer. Add the cream cheese, vanilla and lemon zest. Whip together until fully combined. Add half the icing sugar and mix well. Add the remaining icing sugar and whip together until smooth and white in colour. Set aside.
8. When the cake has fully cooled, spread over the Cream Cheese Icing. Chill to firm up before cutting.
9. Store in an airtight container in the fridge for up to 5 days.

Tips + tricks

+ Neutral oils like canola, sunflower or rice bran work best in this recipe. Strong-flavoured oils such as olive oil will alter the taste of the cake.
+ Make sure the butter and cream cheese are both at room temperature before beating. If they're too cold, the icing will be lumpy.

MASHED POTATO BREAD

You won't believe how soft and fluffy this mashed potato bread is. This is a great way to use up leftover mashed potatoes (if you ever have any!), and makes such a tasty loaf. This is one of the first recipes that went on my website back in 2018 and it's still very popular.

Ready in 2 hours
Makes 2 medium loaves

¼ cup warm water
1 Tbsp active dry yeast
pinch sugar
1 cup boiling water
2 Tbsp butter
2 Tbsp white sugar
1 Tbsp salt
2 cups mashed potatoes
5 cups plain flour

To serve
butter

1. Mix together the warm water and yeast in a small bowl. Add the pinch of sugar to help activate the yeast. Set aside for 10 minutes.
2. Add the boiling water, butter, sugar and salt to the bowl of a stand mixer and stir together until the butter has melted. Add the mashed potatoes and stir with a fork until it has all broken up.
3. Pour in the yeast mixture and add 3 cups of the flour. Attach the dough hook and set the stand mixer to low. Knead until most of the flour is incorporated.
4. Add the remaining flour a cup at a time. Knead on low for 5 minutes until you have a silky dough. If it is too sticky, add more flour a tablespoon at a time. If it is too dry and starting to crack, add water a tablespoon at a time.
5. Remove the dough from the bowl and shape into a ball. Grease the bowl with cooking spray or butter and return the dough. Cover and allow to rise in a warm place for 30 minutes.
6. Grease 2 loaf tins.
7. Punch down the risen dough. Turn out onto a floured surface and knead a few times. Split the dough in half.
8. Divide the dough for each loaf into 3 even portions. Roll each portion into a log, then cross the logs over each other to create a plait. Tuck the ends under the loaf and place in the prepared tins.

Continued overleaf . . .

9. Set aside to rise again in a warm place until almost doubled in size (this usually takes 30–60 minutes). If your kitchen is not warm enough, you can set the oven to the lowest fan bake setting — mine is 40°C (100°F) — and put the dough in there with a bowl of boiling water.
10. Preheat the oven to 180°C (350°F) fan bake.
11. Once the dough has risen, bake for 45 minutes or until golden and cooked through.
12. Remove from the tins and transfer to a baking rack. Slice and serve warm with butter.
13. This loaf is best eaten when fresh but can be stored in an airtight container in the pantry for up to 3 days.

Tips + tricks

+ If you want to make round loaves, shape the dough halves into balls in step 8 and place them onto 2 baking trays lined with baking paper.

NO-BAKE LEMON SLICE

I simply can't get enough of easy no-bake slices. I always end up sneaking to the fridge to grab another small piece. This one is so good thanks to the lemon juice and zest in the base and icing.

Ready in 25 minutes + setting time
Makes 20 pieces

150 g (5½ oz) butter
395 g (14 oz) can sweetened condensed milk
1 cup desiccated coconut
2 × 250 g (9 oz) packets Milk Arrowroot biscuits
zest and juice of 1 lemon (about 2 Tbsp juice)

Lemon Icing
2 cups icing sugar
zest and juice of 1 lemon (about 2 Tbsp juice)
25 g (1 oz) butter, melted

1. Line a 30 × 20 cm (12 × 8 in) slice tin with baking paper.
2. To make the base, add the butter to a large glass bowl and heat in the microwave for 40 seconds until melted. Stir in the condensed milk.
3. Place the coconut and half the biscuits in a food processor and blitz until fine crumbs form. Add to the bowl with the butter mixture.
4. Place the remaining biscuits in the food processor and blitz, but leave larger chunks.
5. Combine all the crushed biscuits and coconut with the butter and condensed milk mixture. Add the lemon zest and juice and mix until well combined.
6. Press into the prepared tin, flattening it down evenly and spreading out to the edges. Chill while you prepare the icing.
7. To make the Lemon Icing, add all the ingredients to a bowl and whisk together until smooth. Spread the icing evenly over the base.
8. Chill for 3+ hours or overnight to set.
9. Once set, cut into pieces. Store in an airtight container in the fridge for up to a week.

Tips + tricks

+ You can use any plain biscuits like Super Wines, Maries, Krispies or Scotch Fingers.

BRIOCHE LOAF

Brioche definitely takes a bit of work to make, but the results are well worth it. I strongly recommend using a stand mixer to create the dough and get the results you want. This delicious dough can be made into one loaf like I have here, or you can slice it into pieces and cook in a muffin tin to make individual scrolls.

Ready in 4 hours
Makes 1 loaf

¼ cup milk, slightly warm
1½ tsp active dry yeast
3 Tbsp white sugar
1 tsp salt
2 eggs
1 tsp vanilla essence
2 cups plain flour
80 g (2¾ oz) butter, softened

Cinnamon Filling

30 g (1 oz) butter, melted
2 tsp vanilla essence
½ cup brown sugar
2 tsp cinnamon
1 Tbsp plain flour
1 cup chocolate drops or chips

To serve

icing sugar (optional)

1. Add the milk, yeast and 1 tablespoon of the sugar to the bowl of a stand mixer. Mix and set aside for about 5 minutes until the yeast is activated and the mixture is foamy.
2. Add the salt, eggs, vanilla and remaining sugar. Sift in the flour. Using a dough hook attachment, mix on a slow speed until the ingredients come together and form a dough.
3. Increase the speed to medium and mix for a further 5 minutes, scraping the sides down as you go.
4. Add half the butter and mix well. Add the remaining butter. Scrape down the sides and pull the dough off the dough hook. Mix on a medium-high speed for a further 5 minutes until all of the butter is incorporated.
5. Turn out onto a well-floured bench and knead a few times into a ball shape. Return to the mixing bowl, cover with cling film and place in a warm area to rise for 2 hours, or store in the fridge overnight.
6. Line a 27 × 13 cm (10¾ × 5 in) loaf tin with baking paper.
7. Turn the dough out onto a well-floured surface and knead for 1 minute. Using a rolling pin and more flour if needed, roll into a large rectangle shape about 5 mm (¼ in) thick. My rectangle was about 50 × 30 cm (20 × 12 in).
8. To make the Cinnamon Filling, mix together the melted butter, vanilla, brown sugar, cinnamon and flour. Spread onto the dough, then scatter with the chocolate drops.

Continued overleaf . . .

9. Starting with the long edge of the rectangle, gently roll the dough into a log. Pinch the edge together to seal the dough.
10. Leaving a 3 cm (1¼ in) length intact at one end, cut through the centre of the roll lengthwise (see photo at top right). Now you should have 2 long pieces that are still connected at one end. Twist the 2 pieces around each other 3–4 times, then pinch the end together. Place in the prepared tin, squeezing the ends in if needed to make it fit. Set aside to rise in a warm spot for about 30 minutes.
11. Preheat the oven to 170°C (325°F) fan bake.
12. Bake for 30–35 minutes or until a skewer inserted into the centre comes out clean.
13. Leave in the tin to cool for 5 minutes, then transfer to a baking rack. Dust with icing sugar (if using) and serve warm. This loaf is best eaten fresh on the day it is made.

Tips + tricks

+ When the dough is being mixed, scrape down the sides as much as you like. The more the better to ensure all the ingredients are incorporated.
+ If you are struggling to roll out the dough and it keeps bouncing back, leave it for 5 minutes and let the dough rest. The gluten will relax and you'll be able to roll the dough much more easily.
+ Microwave the Cinnamon Filling if needed to create a spreadable consistency.
+ To make this into individual scrolls, just slice into 10 pieces after you have rolled up the dough, then bake in muffin tins for 20–25 minutes.

RAW CHOCOLATE SLICE

I love how easy it is to make this raw chocolate slice. You can also roll it into bliss balls if you prefer, but the convenience of the slice is hard to beat! I keep this slice in an airtight container in the fridge so that I can grab a healthyish sweet treat whenever I feel like it.

Ready in 20 minutes + setting time
Makes 12 pieces

1 cup dates
½ cup rolled oats
½ cup desiccated coconut
½ cup cashews
¼ cup cocoa powder
½ cup coconut cream

Dark Chocolate Topping
80 g (2¾ oz) dark chocolate

1. Line a 27 × 13 cm (10¾ × 5 in) loaf tin with baking paper.
2. Place the dates, oats, coconut, cashews, cocoa powder and coconut cream in a food processor and blitz until well combined — some chunks of nuts are fine, though.
3. Pour the mixture into the prepared tin. Push it out to the edges and flatten the top with a spoon.
4. To make the Dark Chocolate Topping, melt the chocolate in the microwave. Spread evenly over the slice.
5. Chill for at least 3 hours or overnight until set, then slice into small bars.
6. Store in an airtight container in the fridge for up to 2 weeks.

Tips + tricks

+ Double this recipe and make it in a larger tin or 2 loaf tins.

TAN SLICE

Tan slice is a retro recipe that many people have great memories of. Some people like to add chocolate chips to their slice. Simply scatter these on top of the caramel with the remaining biscuit topping before the final bake.

Ready in 45 minutes
Makes 16 pieces

200 g (7 oz) butter, softened
½ cup white sugar
½ tsp vanilla essence
½ tsp salt
2¾ cups plain flour
1 tsp baking powder

Caramel Layer
100 g (3½ oz) butter
395 g (14 oz) can sweetened condensed milk
3 Tbsp golden syrup

1. Preheat the oven to 180°C (350°F) fan bake. Line a 27 × 17 cm (10¾ × 6½ in) slice tin with baking paper.
2. To make the base, add the butter, sugar, vanilla and salt to a stand mixer and cream until fluffy and pale in colour. Sift in the flour and baking powder and mix well to combine.
3. Place three-quarters of the base mixture into the prepared tin and smooth down with the back of a metal spoon. Bake for 15 minutes until lightly golden.
4. To make the Caramel Layer, combine all the ingredients in a pot over a medium heat. Stir continuously for about 5 minutes until thickened and a slightly darker colour. Be careful not to burn the caramel — or yourself!
5. Pour the Caramel Layer over the warm base and smooth out evenly. Crumble over the remaining base mixture.
6. Bake for a further 15 minutes or until golden. Set aside to cool.
7. Once cooled, slice into squares. Store in an airtight container in the pantry for up to a week.

Tips + tricks

+ If you want big chunky bits of biscuit dough on the top, squeeze clumps of the base mixture together and scatter them on top of the caramel.
+ If you have a sweet tooth, you can double the Caramel Layer to make it thicker.

PUDDINGS & DESSERTS

WHAT'S IN THIS CHAPTER

Lemon Curd Cheesecake Slice p198

Gingerbread Self-saucing Pudding p200

Chocolate Chip Skillet Cookie p204

Apple Boysenberry Cobbler p206

Pear Crumble p208

Chocolate Self-saucing Pudding p210

STICKY DATE PUDDINGS

Everyone loves this classic dessert. The recipe makes a huge batch of puddings and quite a lot of sauce, too, so you can freeze some for later if you like. The butterscotch sauce will also keep for weeks in the fridge.

Ready in 1 hour 20 minutes
Makes 12 mini puddings

250 g (9 oz) dates, chopped
1 tsp baking soda
1½ cups boiling water
125 g (4½ oz) butter, softened
1 cup brown sugar
1 tsp vanilla essence
2 eggs
½ tsp ground ginger
½ tsp ground allspice
¼ tsp ground nutmeg
1¾ cups plain flour
1½ tsp baking powder

Butterscotch Sauce

2 cups cream
1¼ cups brown sugar
125 g (4½ oz) butter

To serve

ice cream or cream

1. Combine the dates, baking soda and boiling water in a bowl and soak for 20 minutes.
2. Preheat the oven to 175°C (350°F) fan bake. Grease a 12-cup muffin tin.
3. Whisk together the butter, sugar and vanilla in a large bowl. Add the eggs and spices and mix well. Add the date mixture and whisk to combine. Sift in the flour and baking powder and whisk until well combined with no lumps of flour.
4. Pour the mixture into the prepared tin, filling each cup to the top.
5. Bake for 35–45 minutes or until cooked through.
6. To make the Butterscotch Sauce, add all the ingredients to a pot over a medium heat and melt together until beginning to bubble. Simmer for a few minutes while stirring. Remove from the heat and set aside to cool.
7. Serve the puddings warm from the oven, topped with Butterscotch Sauce and a scoop of ice cream or drizzle of cream.

Tips + tricks

+ To make one large pudding, cook in a medium baking dish at 160°C (315°F) fan bake for 45–50 minutes.
+ This makes 12 mini puddings. If you don't need that many, you can halve the recipe (including the Butterscotch Sauce, as that makes enough for all 12 puddings) or freeze any extra puddings in sealable bags for later.

BERRY SELF-SAUCING PUDDING

After the popularity of my Chocolate Self-saucing Pudding (see page 210), I thought it was time to have a berry self-sauce pudding as well, so my sister Grace created this recipe with me. This is a really delicious option for a winter dessert.

Ready in 55 minutes
Serves 6–8

Berry Sauce
1½ cups boiling water
⅔ cup white sugar
1½ cups frozen mixed berries
1 tsp cornflour mixed with 2 Tbsp cold water

80 g (2¾ oz) butter, melted
⅔ cup white sugar
1 egg
1 tsp vanilla essence
¼ tsp salt
¼ cup milk
1 cup plain flour
1 tsp baking powder

To serve
ice cream or cream

1. Preheat the oven to 180°C (350°F) fan bake.
2. To make the Berry Sauce, combine the boiling water, sugar and berries in a pot. If you have any large berries, chop them into smaller pieces. Bring to the boil and dissolve the sugar. Remove from the heat and set aside.
3. Whisk together the melted butter, sugar, egg, vanilla and salt in a mixing bowl for 1 minute. Pour in the milk and sift in the flour and baking powder. Whisk until you have a smooth batter. Spread the batter out evenly in a medium baking dish.
4. Stir the cornflour mixture into the Berry Sauce. Gently pour the sauce over the top of the batter, running it over the back of a large spoon so that the sauce sits on top and doesn't mix into the batter.
5. Bake for 40 minutes or until a skewer inserted into the centre of the cake part comes out clean.
6. Serve warm with a scoop of your favourite ice cream or a drizzle of cream.

Tips + tricks

+ This is best served warm straight from the oven, but you can store it covered in the fridge for up to 3 days and reheat in the microwave.

GOLDEN SYRUP DUMPLINGS

This can be quite a nostalgic dessert for people. These dumplings are soft and fluffy in a beautiful, sticky golden syrup sauce. You can add a sneaky piece of Caramello chocolate inside each dumpling, or keep them traditional if you prefer.

Ready in 1 hour
Serves 6–8

Dumplings

50 g (1¾ oz) butter
⅓ cup golden syrup
½ cup milk, at room temperature
1½ cups plain flour
2 tsp baking powder
10–12 pieces Caramello chocolate

Golden Syrup Sauce

50 g (1¾ oz) butter
1 cup brown sugar
½ cup golden syrup
2 cups boiling water

To serve

vanilla ice cream

1. Preheat the oven to 180°C (350°F) fan bake.
2. To make the Dumplings, add the butter and golden syrup to a large glass bowl and microwave for 45 seconds or until the butter has melted. Pour in the milk and whisk together.
3. Sift in the flour and baking powder. Use a dough whisk or spatula to combine the mixture together. Set aside while you make the sauce.
4. To make the Golden Syrup Sauce, add all the ingredients to an ovenproof frying pan or pot over a low heat. Cook, stirring, until it starts to simmer.
5. Grab a heaped tablespoon of the dough and place a piece of Caramello in the centre. Fold the dough over to enclose the Caramello and roll into a ball. Carefully place the dough ball in the simmering sauce. Repeat until all the dough is used up — it will make about 10–12 dumplings.
6. Turn each dumpling over to coat in the sauce. Simmer for 2 minutes, then transfer the whole pan to the oven.
7. Bake for 15 minutes until the dumplings are cooked through and the sauce has thickened up.
8. Serve warm with ice cream.

Tips + tricks

+ If you prefer, you can roll all your dough balls before you place them in the simmering sauce (step 5), but they're easy to assemble so I just pop them in as I go. It doesn't matter if some of them are sitting in the sauce for a little longer.

Kids' fave

CROISSANT BREAD AND BUTTER PUDDING

If you ever have leftover croissants (hardly ever, right?), this is a great way to use them up. This is a deliciously different way to make bread and butter pudding. The dark chocolate and raspberries complement the flavours so well.

Ready in 50 minutes
Serves 6–8

6 stale croissants
2 Tbsp butter, softened
2 eggs
1 cup milk
1 cup cream
½ tsp cinnamon
¼ cup caster sugar
1 tsp vanilla essence
50 g (1¾ oz) dark chocolate
½ cup frozen raspberries

To serve
1 tsp icing sugar
cream or ice cream

1. Preheat the oven to 180°C (350°F) fan bake. Grease a baking dish.
2. Cut each croissant in half and spread the cut sides with the butter. Arrange the croissant halves side by side in the dish.
3. Whisk together the eggs, milk, cream, cinnamon, sugar and vanilla in a large bowl or jug. Pour the mixture over the croissants, pressing them down slightly to soak.
4. Thinly slice the chocolate with a large sharp knife. Scatter the chocolate and raspberries over the croissants, tucking them between the croissant pieces. Let the mixture soak for 5 minutes.
5. Bake for 30–35 minutes until golden and cooked through.
6. Remove from the oven and allow to sit for 5 minutes.
7. Dust with icing sugar and serve with cream or a scoop of ice cream.

Tips + tricks

+ I like to make this with hot cross buns at Easter.

CLASSIC APPLE PIE

This home-made apple pie is so pretty with its lattice top. Sweet, buttery pastry with a spiced apple filling, served with fresh cream or ice cream to cut through the sweetness . . . this is the ultimate rustic comfort food.

Ready in 1 hour 30 minutes
Serves 8

6 large apples, peeled and diced
3 Tbsp butter
½ cup brown sugar
¼ cup white sugar, plus extra for sprinkling
½ tsp vanilla essence
2 Tbsp plain flour
½ tsp cinnamon
¼ tsp nutmeg
800 g (1 lb 12 oz) sweet shortcrust pastry
1 egg, whisked

To serve
cream or ice cream

1. Preheat the oven to 200°C (400°F) fan bake. Grease a 23 cm (9 in) pie dish.
2. Add the apples, butter, brown sugar and white sugar to a pot and bring to the boil. Cook for 10 minutes or until the apples start to soften.
3. Add the vanilla. Sift in the flour and spices and stir until thickened. Remove from the heat and set aside to cool.
4. Roll out half the pastry and line the pie dish. Spoon in the apple filling.
5. Roll out the remaining pastry and cut into strips. Create a lattice top by weaving the strips together. Brush with the egg wash and sprinkle with some white sugar.
6. Place towards the bottom of the oven and bake for 30–40 minutes.
7. Remove from the oven and allow the pie to cool before slicing. Serve warm or cold with cream or ice cream.

Tips + tricks

+ You can use any of your favourite apples. This recipe was made with slightly tart apples, though, so if you are using a sweet variety you may want to reduce the sugar slightly.

Kids' fave

SNICKERS CHEESECAKE

I love this cheesecake. It is super-versatile so you can use your favourite type of chocolate bar. It's best to set this overnight — it will cut cleanly the next day.

Ready in 30 minutes + setting time
Serves 12

250 g (9 oz) packet malt biscuits
125 g (4½ oz) butter, melted
2 × 44 g (1½ oz) Snickers bars, chopped

Cheesecake Filling

190 g (6¾ oz) milk chocolate, melted
500 g (1 lb 2 oz) cream cheese
¼ cup brown sugar
2 × 44 g (1½ oz) Snickers bars, diced
125 ml (4 fl oz) thickened cream

1. Line the base of a 23 cm (9 in) springform cake tin with baking paper.
2. Place the biscuits in a food processor and blitz to a fine crumb. Add the melted butter and blitz again until combined.
3. Pour the biscuit mixture into the lined tin. Spread out to the edges and push down with the back of a spoon. Place in the fridge to chill.
4. To make the Cheesecake Filling, melt the milk chocolate in a glass bowl in the microwave. Set aside to cool slightly.
5. Place the cream cheese and sugar in the bowl of a stand mixer. Mix together with a paddle attachment on high for a few minutes, scraping down the sides as you go.
6. Add the cooled chocolate to the bowl and mix until incorporated. Add the diced Snickers and mix through. Add the thickened cream and mix for a minute until thick and everything is combined.
7. Pour the filling on top of the chilled base and spread out evenly. Top with the chopped Snickers. Place in the fridge overnight to set completely.
8. Once set, remove from the tin. Carefully remove the baking paper from the base and place on a cake plate. Leave at room temperature to soften for about 20 minutes before slicing and serving.
9. Store in an airtight container in the fridge for up to 3 days.

Tips + tricks

+ Cheesecakes always benefit from a long setting time. If you have to make it on the day you want to serve it, make it as early as possible in the morning.

LEMON CURD CHEESECAKE SLICE

This can be served as a dessert or a treat. It is easy to make and you can easily change up the flavours. Instead of a lemon curd on top you could use ½ cup fruit compote or jam.

Ready in 30 minutes + setting time
Makes 16 pieces

250 g (9 oz) packet malt biscuits
100 g (3½ oz) butter, melted

Lemon Topping

250 ml (9 fl oz) thickened cream
250 g (9 oz) cream cheese, softened
2 Tbsp caster sugar
2 Tbsp lemon juice
½ cup lemon curd

1. Line the base of a 20 cm (8 in) square slice tin with baking paper.
2. To make the base, place the biscuits in a food processor and blitz to a fine crumb. Add the melted butter and blitz again until combined.
3. Pour into the prepared tin. Spread out to the edges and smooth the top with a spatula. Place in the fridge to chill while you make the topping.
4. To make the Lemon Topping, add the thickened cream to the bowl of a stand mixer. Whisk on high for 1 minute until fluffy. Add the cream cheese, sugar, lemon juice and half the lemon curd. Whisk on high for a few minutes until well combined, scraping down the sides as you go.
5. Pour the topping on top of the chilled base and spread out evenly. Dollop the remaining lemon curd over the top and use a spoon to swirl it through. Chill overnight to set completely.
6. Once set, remove from the tin and carefully remove the baking paper from the base. Slice into 16 even pieces using a sharp knife, wiping the knife clean with a paper towel between each slice.
7. Place on a serving plate and serve immediately, or store in an airtight container in the fridge for up to 5 days.

Tips + tricks

+ Thickened cream contains gelatin, which helps the slice to set.
+ Swap the malt biscuits for Milk Arrowroots, Maries, Super Wines or another plain biscuit of your choice.

GINGERBREAD SELF-SAUCING PUDDING

This saucy spiced gingerbread pudding is a quick, no-fuss winter favourite. The pudding comes out fluffy with a gooey ginger caramel sauce underneath. For extra sweet indulgence, top this off with ice cream.

Ready in 1 hour
Serves 6–8

1 cup plain flour
1 tsp baking powder
1 Tbsp ground ginger
2 tsp cinnamon
½ tsp mixed spice
¼ tsp nutmeg
80 g (2¾ oz) butter
3 Tbsp golden syrup
½ cup brown sugar
½ cup milk

Ginger Caramel Sauce
1 tsp cornflour
2 Tbsp cold water
½ cup brown sugar
¼ cup golden syrup
1 Tbsp ground ginger
2 cups boiling water

To serve
icing sugar (optional)
ice cream

1. Preheat the oven to 180°C (350°F) fan bake.
2. Sift the flour, baking powder, ginger, cinnamon, mixed spice and nutmeg into a bowl.
3. Melt the butter, golden syrup and sugar together in a jug in the microwave.
4. Add the milk and the butter mixture to the flour mixture and mix into a smooth batter. Pour into a baking dish and smooth out to the edges.
5. To make the Ginger Caramel Sauce, mix together the cornflour and cold water and combine with the remaining ingredients. Gently pour the sauce over the top of the batter, running it over the back of a large spoon so that the sauce sits on top and doesn't mix into the batter.
6. Bake for about 50 minutes or until a skewer inserted into the centre of the cake part comes out clean.
7. Top with a dusting of icing sugar (if using) and serve warm with ice cream.

Tips + tricks

+ Adjust the spice level to suit you. This recipe is quite strong on ginger so if you are making it for kids I'd recommend cutting the ground ginger quantity in half.

CHOCOLATE CHIP SKILLET COOKIE

There's something special about serving this whole skillet cookie on the table with scoops of ice cream on top and everyone can just dig in. My family and I love doing this and there is usually nothing left at the end. The trick to getting that cute giant cookie look is to add a few chocolate buttons into the soft dough after it is cooked.

Ready in 50 minutes
Serves 6+

150 g (5½ oz) butter, softened
½ cup brown sugar
½ cup caster sugar
1 egg
1 tsp vanilla essence
1½ cups plain flour
½ tsp cinnamon
½ tsp baking soda
3 Tbsp milk
100 g (3½ oz) chocolate buttons

To serve
vanilla ice cream

1. Preheat the oven to 170°C (325°F) fan bake. Grease a 26 cm (10½ in) cast-iron skillet.
2. Add the butter and both sugars to the bowl of a stand mixer and beat until smooth. Add the egg and vanilla and mix on high until pale and fluffy.
3. Sift in the flour, cinnamon and baking soda. Add the milk. Mix on low until just combined.
4. Set aside 15 chocolate buttons for the topping, then chop up the rest and fold through the cookie dough.
5. Press the dough into the skillet and smooth out to the edges.
6. Bake for 25 minutes until just cooked in the centre. Add the reserved chocolate buttons on top.
7. Allow to cool for 10 minutes before serving topped with ice cream.

Tips + tricks

+ This cookie can also be made in a 22 cm (8½ in) round cake tin.
+ You can use milk, dark or white chocolate for this. Buttons, drops, chips or chunks from a block of chocolate will work well, too.
+ You can also cut this into slices to serve (once cooled). You might need to cook it for longer so the centre is slightly firmer.

Kids' fave

APPLE BOYSENBERRY COBBLER

I love a cobbler, and this one is great and so easy. It's like a cake on top of yummy sweet fruit and is a nice option instead of crumble. It also uses canned boysenberries so you can make it all year round.

Ready in 50 minutes
Serves 4

½ cup self-raising flour
½ cup rolled oats
½ cup white sugar
1 tsp cinnamon
½ cup milk
50 g (1¾ oz) butter, melted
2 apples, peeled and thinly sliced
425 g (15 oz) can boysenberries

To serve
icing sugar (optional)
ice cream
cream

1. Preheat the oven to 180°C (350°F) fan bake.
2. Stir together the flour, oats, sugar and cinnamon. Pour in the milk and melted butter and mix to combine.
3. Add the apples to a baking dish. Drain half the liquid from the can of boysenberries, then stir in the rest with the apples. Cover with the batter.
4. Bake in the oven for 30–40 minutes until golden and cooked through.
5. Dust with icing sugar (if using) and serve warm with ice cream or cream — or both!

Tips + tricks

+ Feel free to use a combination of your favourite fresh, frozen or canned fruits in this dessert.

PEAR CRUMBLE

Sometimes it's nice to mix it up so instead of the classic apple crumble, I've made a pear version. This is absolutely delicious served with custard and/or ice cream.

Ready in 50 minutes
Serves 6

2 Tbsp butter
2 Tbsp brown sugar
4 pears, peeled and thinly sliced
2 Tbsp water

Crumble Topping
100 g (3½ oz) butter, melted
100 g (3½ oz) brown sugar
1 cup rolled oats
110 g (3¾ oz) plain flour
½ tsp cinnamon

To serve
custard and/or ice cream

1. Preheat the oven to 180°C (350°F) fan bake.
2. Melt the butter in a pot over a low heat. Add the sugar and mix together for a few minutes until bubbling.
3. Add the pears and stir to coat. Add the water and simmer for 5 minutes until the pears start to soften. Remove from the heat and transfer the mixture to a baking dish.
4. To make the Crumble Topping, stir together the melted butter and sugar in a large bowl. Add the oats, flour and cinnamon and mix until well combined. Spread evenly over the top of the pears.
5. Bake for 30 minutes or until crisp and golden.
6. Serve warm with custard and/or ice cream.

Tips + tricks

+ Swap the pears for apples, chopped rhubarb, feijoas, frozen berries or stone fruit.

CHOCOLATE SELF-SAUCING PUDDING

Everyone loves a classic chocolate self-sauncing pudding. For my husband Mike and the boys, this is the ultimate dessert. I hope it becomes a favourite in your house, too.

Ready in 45 minutes
Serves 6

50 g (1¾ oz) butter, cubed
½ cup milk
1 egg
½ cup white sugar
1 cup plain flour
1 tsp baking powder
2 Tbsp cocoa powder

Chocolate Sauce
½ cup brown sugar
3 Tbsp cocoa powder
1 Tbsp cornflour
1½–2 cups boiling water

To serve
ice cream, custard or whipped cream

1. Preheat the oven to 180°C (350°F) fan bake. Grease a baking dish.
2. Add the butter to a large glass bowl and melt in the microwave. Add the milk and egg and whisk together. Add the sugar and whisk again.
3. Sift in the flour, baking powder and cocoa. Fold together until just combined. Pour into the prepared dish and spread to the edges.
4. To make the Chocolate Sauce, add the sugar, cocoa and cornflour to a glass jug and stir to combine. Pour in the boiling water and mix until the sugar has dissolved. Gently pour the sauce over the top of the batter, running it over the back of a large spoon so that the sauce sits on top and doesn't mix into the batter.
5. Bake for 25–30 minutes or until the pudding springs back when lightly touched.
6. Serve warm with ice cream, custard or whipped cream.

Tips + tricks

+ I sometimes add a mashed banana to the batter to mix up the flavour.

Kids' fave

Corona
Extra

ACKNOWLEDGEMENTS

Thank you so much for buying this book! If you've already purchased one or both of my other books, I hope you've enjoyed them as much as I know you'll enjoy this one. Your support means the world to me, whether it's from buying my books, following me on Instagram or Facebook, or using recipes from my app or website.

A big thanks goes out to my whānau. My supportive husband, Mike, celebrates every milestone with me. From publishing a new book to growing the business, he's always by my side. To my wonderful sisters, Gemma, Holly and Grace, and my brother, Alex: it was awesome to have you join in the photoshoot at home, gathering around the fire for good times.

A special mention goes to my sister Grace, an amazing baker who's been a key part of the team for the past few years. Your knowledge of baking science is invaluable. Thank you for contributing some of the sweet treats in this book, including the sticky date and gingerbread puddings. It was so special to take photos of Grace while she was pregnant with my beautiful niece, Cleo.

I'm so grateful to my mum, Margot, and her partner, Rob, for always cheering me on from Raglan. My dad, Paul, and his partner, Lyndal, are also huge supporters. Dad has got into cooking and sends me photos of what he makes; he's particularly fond of the hearty beef stew from *Everyday Favourites*. My supportive in-laws, Mark and Barb, love showing off my books to their friends.

To my friends in Taupō: thank you for the constant support and laughs — it's been fun hosting you in my new studio space. And to my food blogger friends: I really appreciate the time we spend together on our foodie retreats. I always come away so inspired.

I know how lucky I am to have my incredible team. Theresa and Erin H, you make the office such a fun place to be, and you keep me grounded when I come up with wild ideas! Erin S, Jane and Holly, thank you for your hard work and big smiles.

Shooting this cookbook with Lottie in Taupō was a highlight again this year. I loved showcasing the local rivers and landscapes. Archie and Henry had fun searching for trees with golden leaves, and Mike even caught a fish on cue — perfect timing!

Shooting the recipe photos in Auckland was a blast, too. Mel and Jo, you guys really are the dream team, and I'm so happy with how the cosy, moody winter shots turned out. Huge thanks to Theresa and Erin H for coming up and helping in the studio — ten recipes a day is no small feat, especially with all the dishes!

A big thank you to Allen & Unwin: Miff, Leanne, Jenny and the whole team. I appreciate your trust in me to create these beautiful books. Special thanks to Kate Barraclough for your brilliant design work, and to Kate Grimstock and the proofreaders who comb through my words again and again.

Finally, thanks once more to you, my readers. I hope this book is well used in your kitchen and becomes your winter food bible, splattered with slow-cooked sauce.

Vanya x

INDEX

T

V

W

Y

Photography Credits

Lottie Hedley front cover, back flap, pages 2–11, 14–15, 30–31, 42–43, 52–53, 74–75, 96–97, 104–105, 118–119, 129, 146–147, 158–159, 167, 173, 178–179, 192–193, 202–203, 212–216, 222–223

Melanie Jenkins (Flash Studios) back cover, front flap, pages 13, 16–29, 33–41, 45–51, 55–73, 77–95, 99–103, 107–117, 121–127, 131–145, 149–157, 161–165, 169–171, 175–177, 180–191, 195–201, 205–211, 221, 224

muesli

Note: Vanya uses New Zealand standard measures, including the 15 ml (3 teaspoon) tablespoon. If you are using the Australian 20 ml (4 teaspoon) tablespoon, you may wish to remove a teaspoon of ingredient for each tablespoon specified.

First published in 2025

Recipe styling by Jo Bridgford (Delivision Food Styling)

See page 220 for photography credits by page

Allen & Unwin
Level 2, 10 College Hill, Freemans Bay
Auckland 1011, New Zealand
Phone: (64 9) 377 3800
Email: auckland@allenandunwin.com
Web: www.allenandunwin.co.nz

83 Alexander Street
Crows Nest NSW 2065, Australia
Phone: (61 2) 8425 0100

A catalogue record for this book is available from the National Library of New Zealand.

ISBN 978 1 991006 42 4

Special thanks to Isness Ceramics, Acme Cupco, and Delivision Food & Prop Styling

Design by Kate Barraclough
Set in Neue Haas Unica W1 and TT Ramillas
Printed in China by 1010 Printing Limited

10 9 8 7 6 5 4 3 2 1

MIX
Paper | Supporting responsible forestry
FSC® C016973
FSC www.fsc.org